At a Glance

Essays

Lee Brandon
Mt. San Antonio College

Houghton Mifflin Company   *Boston   New York*

Senior Sponsoring Editor: Mary Jo Southern
Senior Associate Editor: Ellen Darion
Editorial Assistant: Kate O'Sullivan
Senior Project Editor: Kathryn Dinovo
Senior Manufacturing Coordinator: Sally Culler
Senior Marketing Manager: Nancy Lyman

Cover design and image: Henry Rachlin

To Sharon

Printed in the U.S.A.

Library of Congress Catalog Card Number: 98-71997

ISBN: 0-395-91869-3

23456789-DH-02 01 00 99

Contents

4 *Descriptive Narration: Moving Through Time and Space*   51

5 *Exemplification: Writing with Examples*   67

8 *Cause and Effect: Determining Reasons and Results*   *103*

9 *Classification: Establishing Groups*   *118*

Appendix B   *Handbook*   *192*

Text Credits   *215*

Index   *217*

Preface

At a Glance: Essays is the third-level book in the new *At a Glance* series of concise writing handbooks. Along with *At a Glance: Sentences* and *At a Glance: Paragraphs*, it meets the current need for succinct, comprehensive, and up-to-date textbooks that students can afford. All three books provide basic instruction, exercises, and writing assignments at the designated level, as well as support material for instructors. *At a Glance: Sentences* and *At a Glance: Paragraphs* include a transition to the next level of writing while *At a Glance: Paragraphs* and *At a Glance: Essays* end with a handbook, to which students can refer for help with sentence-level issues or for problems with mechanics. Each book in the *At a Glance* series can be used alone, as part of a two- or three-level sequence, or as a supplement to another type of textbook used in the course.

COMPREHENSIVE COVERAGE

Focusing on essay writing, *At a Glance: Essays* covers prewriting techniques, first drafts, revising, and editing—each phase illustrated with student examples. The book then presents nine patterns of essay writing, with a chapter devoted to each: descriptive narration, exemplification, analysis by division, process analysis, cause and effect, classification, comparison and contrast, definition, and argument.

Appendix A, "The Research Paper," includes forms of documentation as well as a discussion of libraries, on-line searching, plagiarism, and other research-related topics. *At a Glance: Essays* concludes with a handbook that covers sentence-level issues (subjects and predicates, fragments, coordination and subordination, and so on); specific verb, pronoun, and modifier problems; and punctuation and capitalization.

INSTRUCTIONAL APPROACH

The instruction in *At a Glance: Essays* is concise and direct, using thought-provoking example essays, hands-on exercises, and writing practice. Chapters 4 through 12 each present writing strategies for a particular essay pattern, followed by an annotated student example, a professional example with questions for students to answer, an exercise that gives students practice in organizing the pattern, topics (reading-related, career-related, and general) for writing such essays, and a summary of guidelines specific to the pattern.

SUPPORT MATERIAL FOR INSTRUCTORS

- *Instructor's Guide.*   Provides answers to exercises, a diagnostic test, a final test, and three quizzes for each major unit. Quizzes may be photocopied and distributed to students as additional classroom exercises.
- *English Microlab* for PC and Macintosh.   Teaches and reinforces the basics of grammar, punctuation, and mechanics. An accompanying data disk allows instructors to manage and record group results.
- *Expressways,* Second Edition, for PC, Macintosh, and Windows.   Interactive software that guides students as they write and revise paragraphs and essays.

ACKNOWLEDGMENTS

I am profoundly indebted to the following instructors who have reviewed this textbook: Marilyn Black, Middlesex Community College; Deborah Burson-Smith, Southern University at New Orleans; David Lang, Golden Gate University; Kathy Masters, Arkansas State University; and Steve Stremmel, American River College. Thanks also to members of the English department at Mt. San Antonio College, with special recognition to the Basic Courses Review Committee.

I deeply appreciate the work of freelance editor Marilyn Weissman, as well as that of my colleagues at Houghton Mifflin: Mary Jo Southern, Ellen Darion, Kate O'Sullivan, Nancy Lyman, and Henry Rachlin.

For their cheerful, inspiring presence, I am especially grateful to my wife, my children and their spouses, and my grandchildren: Sharon, Kelly, Erin, Jeanne, Michael, Shane, Lauren, and Jarrett.

Lee Brandon

Student Overview

This book is designed to help you write better essays. Chapter 1 defines the essay and discusses what you need to know and do to write effective essays. Chapters 2 and 3 focus on the writing process itself—how to get started and how to develop, revise, and edit your working drafts. Every stage is illustrated by the work of one student, whom we follow through the entire process.

Chapters 4 through 12 each describe a different pattern for developing an essay. For example, Chapter 4, "Descriptive Narration," is about writing an essay by using both description and storytelling techniques. Chapter 5, "Exemplification," is about writing an essay by using examples. Chapters 4 through 12 all include an essay written by a student and one written by a professional writer. In every chapter, questions and exercises help you put into practice what you have learned.

Appendix A is about writing the research paper and the special considerations that kind of essay involves. Finally, the book ends with Appendix B, a Handbook, to which you can refer whenever you need assistance in grammar, usage, punctuation, and capitalization.

Below are some strategies you can follow to make the best use of this book and to jump-start the improvement in your writing skills.

1. **Be Active and Systematic in Learning.** Take advantage of your instructor's expertise by being an active class member—one who takes notes, asks questions, and contributes to discussion. Become dedicated to systematic learning: determine your needs, decide what to do, and do it. Make learning a part of your everyday thinking and behavior.
2. **Read widely.** Samuel Johnson, a great English scholar, once said that he didn't want to read anything by people who had written more than they had read. William Faulkner, a Nobel Prize winner in literature, said, "Read, read, read. Read everything—trash, classics, good and bad, and see how writers do it." Read to learn technique, to acquire ideas, to be stimulated to write. Especially read to satisfy your curiosity and to receive pleasure. If reading is a main component of your course, approach it as systematically as you do writing.
3. **Keep a Journal.** Keeping a journal may not be required in your particular class, but whether required or not, it is a good idea to

jot down your own ideas. Here are some topics for daily, or regular, journal writing:

- Summarize, evaluate, or react to reading assignments.
- Summarize, evaluate, or react to what you see on television and in movies, and to what you read in newspapers and in magazines.
- Describe and narrate situations or events you experience.
- Write about career-related matters you encounter in other courses or on the job.

Your journal entries may read like an intellectual diary, a record of what you are thinking about at certain times. Because your entries are not structured writing assignments, organization and editing are not important. Mainly, keeping a journal will help you understand the material you read, develop your language skills, think more clearly, become more confident, and write more easily so that writing itself becomes a comfortable everyday activity. Your entries may also provide subject material for longer, more carefully crafted pieces.

The most important thing is to get into the habit of writing something each day.

4. **Evaluate your writing skills.** Use the Self-Evaluation Chart inside the front cover of this book to list areas you need to work on. You can add to your lists throughout the entire term. Drawing on your instructor's comments, make notes on matters such as the organization, development, and content of your essays; spelling, vocabulary, and diction; and so on. Use the chart for self-motivated study assignments and as a checklist in all stages of writing. As you master each problem area, you can check it off or cross it out.

Opposite is a partially filled out Self-Evaluation Chart, with some guidelines for filling out your own.

Organization/Development/Content: Note your instructor's suggestions for all aspects of planning your essays and supporting your ideas.

Spelling/Word Choice: List words marked as incorrectly spelled on your assignments. Master the words on your list and add new words as you accumulate assignments. List suggestions made by your instructor about word choice (such as avoiding slang, clichés, and vague terms). Also include new, useful words you encounter in this class and others; add the words here, with simple definitions. Use another page if you need more space.

Self-Evaluation Chart

Organization/ Development/ Content	Spelling/ Word Choice	Grammar/ Sentences	Punctuation/ Capitalization
Avoid top-heavy introductions 9 Use specific examples 67 Repeat key words such as *causes* and *effects*	all right separate sophomore avoid "into" as "into rap" "couldn't care less" 32	Vary sentence beginnings 193 Watch for pronoun antecedent problems, such as "a person . . . they" 205 RO/CS—*Then* isn't a conjunction 195	comma after long introductory mod. 208 colon to introduce list 211 cap beginning for words replacing names, such, "I told Mother," but "I told my mother" 213

Grammar/Sentences: List any grammar points you need to remember or any sentence problems, such as fragments, comma splices, and run-ons. If you tend to begin sentences in the same way or to use the same patterns, use your chart to remind yourself to vary your sentence beginnings and patterns.

Punctuation/Capitalization: List any problems you encounter with punctuation or capitalization. Because the items in this column may be covered in the Handbook at the end of this book, you can often use both rule numbers and page numbers for the references here.

5. **Be positive.** To improve your English skills, write with freedom—but revise and edit with rigor. Work with your instructor to set attainable goals, and proceed at a reasonable pace. Your Self-Evaluation Chart will give you direction and focus. Seeing what you have mastered and checked off your list will give you a sense of accomplishment.

   Don't compare yourself with others. Compare yourself with yourself, and as you make progress, consider yourself what you are—a student on the path toward effective writing, a student on the path of success.

1

The Essay and Its Parts

THE ESSAY DEFINED

An essay is a group of paragraphs, each of which supports a controlling idea called a thesis. The number of paragraphs in an essay varies, but in college writing that number is likely to be between three and nine. Many college essays are about five paragraphs long, often because of the nature of the assignment and the length of time allowed, but there is no special significance in the number five.

Each paragraph in an essay is almost always one of three types:

1. The introductory paragraph presents the thesis, the controlling idea of the essay, much as a topic sentence presents the main idea of a paragraph.
2. The paragraphs in the body of the essay present evidence and reasoning—the support for the thesis of the essay.
3. The concluding paragraph provides an appropriate ending—often a restatement of or reflection on the thesis.

Thus a typical essay has this basic form, though the number of support paragraphs may vary:

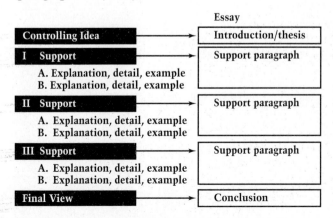

1

A Sample Essay

The following essay was written by Leah, an inmate at a women's prison in California who enrolled in a small, low-cost college program. The parts of her essay are marked to show the organization of the paragraphs. Though only the final draft appears here, Leah's essay also provides the examples for the stages and techniques of the writing process discussed in Chapters 2 and 3.

Razor Wire Sweat Lodge

Leah

Introductory paragraph My Indian tribe is Pomo, one of twenty-one represented at this prison. I have always had tremendous interest in my ancestors and their customs, and in the cultures of all Indian tribes. The sacred sweat ceremony itself is at the center of my life. Here at prison it has taken on a special meaning. In fact, many women of other races here have also found peace within themselves as a result of participating with me and other **Thesis** Native Americans in the sweats. Each Saturday we have a routine: we make preparations, we sweat, and we conclude with a post-sweat activity.

Topic sentence Before we sweat, we must prepare ourselves and the facility. For twenty-four hours before the sweat, we fast. We do not eat anything and drink only water or juices, but if someone has a health problem, we will excuse her. As for clothing we wear simple, loose dresses such as the prison-issued muu-muus. We bring tobacco ties, sage leaves, sweet grass, and sometimes a pipe. Preparing the facility is more complicated than preparing ourselves. About thirty-five lava rocks must be heated in a fire approximately three hours before we start sweating. The wood for the fire has to be placed in a tepee **Support** shape around the pile of rocks and ignited. **paragraph 1** Once the fire is hot, we tend to the sweat lodge itself. Since we have no tarp to put on the sweat lodge frame, the state provides us with blankets. We use these to cover the lodge fully, draping it with about three layers and leaving an opening to the east. Finally we are ready to go inside. The preparation period is very important, but everyone looks forward to its being over.

Topic From this point on through the ceremony, **sentence** everything must be done according to rules. First we enter counterclockwise, and once inside we conduct all parts of the ceremony counterclockwise. There are four rounds in the sweat, each of which lasts about twenty to thirty minutes. We stress that no one should break our circle inside the sweat **Support** lodge, but it sometimes happens. Some women **paragraph**

can't handle the steam and the heat, so we never make them stay. Those who do stay are free to participate in the singing and praying or not. The four rounds are similar. For each, six hot rocks are brought in, and six dippers of water are poured onto the rocks. The number six indicates the four directions and the sky and the ground. As someone finishes a prayer (usually in Sioux because our sponsor is a Sioux), she mentions her relatives, for this ceremony is also for others. Then another person follows. As sweet grass burns outside on the fire, we sit in the hot steam and rub sage leaves on our bodies for purification. We maintain ourselves with humility during the whole sweat.

Topic sentence

When the sweat is over, we enter the final phase. We come out and throw our tobacco ties into the fire pit, and the smoke takes our prayers to the sky. Then we hose ourselves down with plenty of cold water and open the refreshments we brought. Once we've eaten and changed our clothes, we start dismantling the sweat. The blankets have to be taken off the same way they were put up and then folded carefully. The leftover wood has to be put away, and the blankets and wood

Support paragraph

must be covered. Any garbage that's been left
around is thrown into the Dumpster. Then we
lock the gate to our facility and bid
farewell.

Concluding paragraph
Using a sweat lodge is a custom of most
Indian tribes. Certain Indian tribes go about
it differently from others, but in here when
we are together in the lodge, we feel like
one whole being. Each week we look forward to
this ceremony. It helps us cope better with
the prison system. After it's over, we feel
physically refreshed, clean, and peaceful.

THE THESIS DEFINED

If you tell a friend you are about to write an essay, be prepared for
the question, "What are you writing about?" If you answer, "Public
schools," your friend will probably be satisfied with the answer but
not very interested. The problem is that the phrase *public schools*
doesn't suggest a focus or direction. It just indicates your subject,
not what you are going to do with it. An effective controlling statement, called the *thesis of the essay*, has both a *subject* and a *treatment*. The *subject* is what you intend to write about. The *treatment* is what you intend to do with your subject.

Glendora High School offers a well-balanced academic program.
subject   treatment

SOURCES FOR THE THESIS

The thesis of an essay can come from any of several places. You
may generate it early on through prewriting techniques, you may
develop it from something you have read, or you may be assigned a
topic. In any case, you need to work on your thesis statement—just
that one sentence—until you have developed an interesting subject
and a well-focused treatment. Your working thesis may be a bit dif-

ferent from the one you finally use in your essay, but it can easily be reworded once you begin writing and revising.

WRITING THE THESIS

An effective thesis includes a treatment that can be developed with supporting information. An ineffective statement presents a treatment that is vague, too broad, or too narrow.

> VAGUE   <u>Public schools</u> <u>are great.</u>
>   subject   treatment
>
> BETTER   <u>Public schools</u> <u>do as well academically as private</u>
>   subject   treatment
> <u>schools, according to statistics.</u>
> (made more specific)
>
> TOO BROAD   <u>Public schools</u> <u>are having trouble.</u>
>   subject   treatment
> (trouble with what?)
>
> BETTER   <u>Bidwell Elementary School</u> <u>is too crowded.</u>
>   subject   treatment
> (limiting the idea of trouble)
>
> ·TOO NARROW   <u>American public schools</u> <u>were first established</u>
>   subject   treatment
> <u>in Philadelphia in 1779.</u> (only a fact)

EXERCISE 1

In the following theses, underline and label the subjects (S) and treatments (T). Also judge each one as E (effective) or I (ineffective).

EXAMPLE:

                    S   T

_____I_____   <u>Basketball</u>   <u>is an interesting sport.</u>

_____   1. Students who cheat in school may be trying to relieve certain emotional pressures.

_____   2. Shakespeare was an Elizabethan writer.

_____   3. The quarterback in football and the general of an army are alike in significant ways.

_____   4. Animals use color chiefly for protection.

_____ 5. Portland is a city in Oregon.

_____ 6. Life in the ocean has distinct realms.

_____ 7. Rome has had a glorious and tragic history.

_____ 8. Boston is the capital of Massachusetts.

_____ 9. The word *macho* has a special meaning to the Hispanic community.

_____ 10. The history of plastics is exciting.

EXERCISE 2

Convert each of the following subjects into an effective thesis.

1. Bumper stickers _____

   _____

2. Rudeness _____

   _____

3. The true character of my neighbor _____

   _____

4. Many homeless people _____

   _____

5. Being able to use a computer_____

   _____

6. Dieting _____

   _____

7. The basic forms of jazz and classical music _____

   _____

8. Educated citizens _____

   _____

9. The required labeling of rock music albums _____

_____

10. Smoking _____

_____

PATTERNS OF SUPPORT FOR THE THESIS

If the foundation of an effective essay is a strong thesis—one with a specific subject and a well-defined treatment—the strength of the essay is in the support. Whether that support comes from research or personal experience, it will almost certainly be suggested by the treatment imposed on the subject. After settling on a thesis, you should pose two questions:

1. What kinds of information will best support or explain my thesis?
2. How should I divide and present that supporting information?

The way you choose to divide and present your information will determine the organization of your support paragraphs.

Among the most common forms of dividing and organizing ideas are these:

- Narration (telling a story)

    Division: parts of the story

    I. Situation
    II. Conflict
    III. Struggle
    IV. Outcome
    V. Meaning

- Analysis by division: (examining the parts of a unit; for example, a pencil can be divided into an eraser, a wooden barrel, and a lead core with a point at the end)

    Division: parts of the unit

    I. First part
    II. Second part
    III. Third part

- Process analysis: (how to do something or how something was done)

Division: preparation and steps

    I. Preparation
    II. Steps
        A. Step 1
        B. Step 2
        C. Step 3
        D. Step 4

- Cause and effect

Division: causes or effects (sometimes mixed)

    I. Cause (or effect) one
    II. Cause (or effect) two
    III. Cause (or effect) three

Other patterns of developing an essay include classification, comparison and contrast, definition, and argumentation. All of these forms are presented individually in Chapters 4 through 12. Although a single form is often dominant at either the paragraph or short essay level, a rich combination of forms is common.

SPECIAL PARAGRAPHS WITHIN THE ESSAY

Introductions

A good introductory paragraph does many things. It attracts the reader's interest, states or points toward the thesis, and moves the reader smoothly into the support, or body, paragraphs. Here are some introductory methods:

- A direct statement of the thesis
- Background
- Definition of term(s)
- Quotation(s)
- A shocking statement
- Question(s)
- A combination of two or more methods on this list

You should not decide that some of the methods are good and some are bad. Indeed, all are valid, and the most common one is the last, the combination. Use the approach that best fits each essay. Resist the temptation to use the same kind of introduction in every essay you write.

The thesis is the same in all of the introductory paragraphs below, yet each uses a different introductory method. Notice the great variety here.

Direct Statement of Thesis

SUBJECT TREATMENT

Anyone on the road in any city near midnight on Friday and Saturday is among dangerous people. They're not the product of the witching hour; they're the product of the "happy hour." They're called drunk drivers. These threats to our lives and limbs need to be controlled by federal laws with strong provisions.

Background

SUBJECT TREATMENT

In one five-year period in California (1993–1997), 227,000 people were injured and 47,000 were killed by drunk drivers. Each year, the same kinds of figures come in from all our states. The state laws vary. The federal government does virtually nothing. Drunk driving has reached the point of being a national problem of huge proportions. This slaughter of innocent citizens should be stopped by following the lead of many other nations and passing federal legislation with strong provisions.

Definition

SUBJECT TREATMENT

Here's a recipe. Take two thousand pounds of pastic, rubber, and steel, pour in ten gallons of gas, and start the engine. Then take one human being of one hundred to two hundred pounds of flesh, blood, and bones, pour in two glasses of beer in one hour, and put him or her behind the wheel. Mix the two together, and the result may be a drunken driver ready to cause death and destruction. This problem of drunk driving can and should be controlled by federal legislation with strong provisions.

Quotation

The National Highway Traffic Safety Administration says more than 50 percent of all fatal accidents involve intoxicated drivers and about "75 percent of those drivers have a blood alcohol content of .10 percent or greater." That kind of information is widely known, yet the carnage on the highways continues. <u>This problem of drunk driving</u> should be addressed by a federal law with strict provisions.

SUBJECT
TREATMENT

Shocking Statement and Questions

Almost 60,000 Americans were killed in the Vietnam War. What other war kills more than that number each year? Give up? It's the war with drunk drivers. The war in Vietnam ended about two decades ago, but our DUI war goes on, and the drunks are winning. <u>This deadly conflict</u> should b controlled by a federal law with strong provisions.

SUBJECT
TREATMENT

Questions and a Definition

What is a drunk driver? In California it's a person with a blood alcohol content of .08 percent or more who is operating a motor vehicle. What do those drivers do? Some of them kill. Every year more than 60,000 people nationwide die. Those are easy questions. The difficult one is, What can be done? One answer is clear: <u>drunk drivers</u> should be controlled by federal laws with strong provisions.

SUBJECT
TREATMENT

All these introductory methods are effective. Some others, however, are ineffective because they are too vague to carry the thesis or because they carry the thesis in a mechanical way. The mechanical approach may be direct and explicit, but it usually destroys the reader's imagination and interest.

AVOID   The purpose of this essay is to write about the need for strong national laws against drunk driving.

AVOID   I will now write a paper about the need for strong national laws against drunk driving.

The length of an introduction can vary, but the typical length for a student essay is three to five sentences. If your introduction is shorter than three, be certain that it conveys all that you want to say. If it is longer than five, be certain that it only introduces and does not try to expand on ideas. That function is reserved for the body paragraphs; a long and complicated introduction may make your essay top-heavy.

EXERCISE 3

Pick one of the following theses (altering it a bit to suit your own ideas, if you like) and write two different introductory paragraphs for it, each one featuring a different method. Underline the thesis in each paragraph, and label the subject and treatment parts.

1. Marriages come in different shapes and sizes.
2. Career choices are greatly influenced by a person's background.
3. *Friendship* is just one word, but friends are of different kinds.
4. The spirit of sports has been corrupted by money.
5. Sexual harassment at work often goes unreported for practical reasons.

Conclusions

Your concluding paragraph should give the reader the feeling that you have said all you want to say about your subject. Like introductory paragraphs, concluding paragraphs are of various types. Here are some effective ways of concluding a paper:

- Conclude with a final paragraph or sentence that is a logical part of the body of the paper; that is, it functions as part of the support. In the following example, there is no formal conclusion. This form is more common in the published essay than in the student essay.

> **Maria** One day he hit me. He said he was sorry and even cried,
> **Campos,** but I could not forgive him. We got a divorce. It took me
> **"A Divorce** a while before I could look back and see what the causes
> **with Reasons"** really were, but by then it was too late to make any
> changes.

- Conclude with a restatement of the thesis in slightly different words, perhaps pointing out its significance and/or making applications.

Norman Cousins, "Who Killed Benny Paret?"	Don't blame it on the referee. Don't even blame it on the fight managers. Put the blame where it belongs—on the prevailing mores that regard prize fighting as a perfectly proper enterprise and vehicle of entertainment. No one doubts that many people enjoy prize fighting and will miss it if it should be thrown out. And that is precisely the point.

- Conclude with a review of the main points of the discussion—a kind of summary. This is appropriate only if the complexity of the essay makes a summary necessary.

Carl Wingus, "Conserving Energy as You Ski"	As we have been made all too aware lately in this country, the more energy we conserve now, the more we'll have for the future. The same holds true for skiing. So take the Soft Path of energy conservation as you ski. You'll not only be able to make longer nonstop runs, but you'll have more energy to burn on the dance floor.

- Conclude with an anecdote related to the thesis.

Brian Maxwell, "Leaving Los Angeles"	Over the harsh traffic sounds of motors and horns and blaring radios came the faint whang-whang of a would-be musician with a beat-up guitar and a money-drop hat turned up at his feet. It all reminded me of when I had first experienced the conglomeration of things that now assailed my senses. This jumbled mixture of things both human and nonhuman was, in fact, the reason I had come to live here. Then it was different and exciting. Later it was the reason I was leaving.

- Conclude with a quotation related to the thesis.

Daniel Humphries, "Get Them Off the Road"	More than half the fatal traffic accidents involve intoxicated drivers, according to the National Highway Traffic Safety Administration. Cavenaugh and Associates, research specialists, say that drunk drivers killed 47,000 people in California in the five-year period from 1993 through 1997. They go on to say that intoxicated drivers cost us somewhere between eleven billion and twenty-four billion dollars each year. It is time to give drunk drivers a message: "Stay off the road. You are costing us pain, injury, and death, and no one has the right to do that."

There are also many ineffective ways of concluding a paper. Do not conclude with the following:

- a summary when a summary is unnecessary.
- a complaint about the assignment or an apology about the quality of the work.
- an afterthought—that is, something you forgot to discuss in the body of the paper.
- a tagged conclusion—that is, a sentence beginning with such phrases as *In conclusion, To conclude,* or *I would like to conclude this discussion,* or *Last but not least.*
- a conclusion that raises additional problems that should have been settled during the discussion.

The conclusion is an integral part of the essay and is often a reflection of the introduction. If you have trouble with the conclusion, reread your introduction. Then work for a roundness or completeness in the whole paper.

EXERCISE 4

For Exercise 3, you wrote two introductions. Select the better one, consider the basic information you would probably use for support (jotting down a few ideas if you like), and then write a simple conclusion of three to five sentences. This is only an exercise to demonstrate that the conclusion connects with the introduction, is a consequence of the development of the essay, and ends on a note of finality. Of course, in your regular assignments, you will not write your conclusion until after you have written the other paragraphs.

WRITER'S GUIDELINES AT A GLANCE: THE ESSAY AND ITS PARTS

1. An essay is a group of paragraphs, each of which supports a controlling statement called a thesis.
2. Each paragraph in an essay is almost always one of three types: introductory, support, or concluding.
3. An effective thesis has both a subject and a treatment.

   The subject is what you intend to write about.
   The treatment is what you intend to do with your subject.

   EXAMPLE: <u>Bidwell Elementary School</u> <u>is too crowded.</u>
                           subject   statement

4. An effective thesis presents a treatment that can be developed with supporting information.

5. An ineffective thesis is vague, too broad, or too narrow.
6. Supporting information is often presented in patterns, such as narration, cause and effect, analysis by division, and process analysis.
7. A good introductory paragraph attracts the reader's interest, states or points toward the thesis, and moves the reader smoothly into the support, or body, paragraphs.
8. Introductory methods include a direct statement of the thesis, background, definition of term(s), quotation(s), a shocking statement, question(s), and a combination of two or more methods in this list.
9. Your concluding paragraph should give the reader the feeling that you have said all you want to say about your subject.
10. Some effective methods of concluding are a restatement of the thesis in slightly different words, perhaps pointing out its significance or making applications of it; a review of the main points; an anecdote related to the thesis; and a quotation.

2

The Writing Process: Prewriting

Chapter 1 focused on organizing and writing an essay. However, it stopped short of presenting an overall plan for completing a specific writing assignment. The reason for that omission is simple. Each assignment has its own guidelines that vary according to the kind of topic, the source of ideas, the time permitted, the conditions for writing (especially in or outside class), and the purpose. Obviously, if one is to use a system, it must be flexible, because a technique that is an asset for one assignment may be a burden for another. Therefore, a good writer should know numerous techniques, treating each as a tool that can be used when needed. All of these tools are in the same box, one labeled "The Writing Process."

THE WRITING PROCESS DEFINED

The writing process consists of strategies that can help you proceed from your purpose or initial idea to a final developed essay. Those strategies can be divided into prewriting techniques and writing stages. Using prewriting techniques, you explore, experiment, gather information, formulate your thesis, and develop and organize your support. In the writing stages, you write a first draft, revise your draft as many times as necessary, and edit your writing. For the typical college writing assignment, the writing process looks like this:

Prewriting

- Exploring, experimenting, gathering information
- Writing the controlling idea, organizing and developing support

Writing

- Drafting, revising, editing

Prewriting is discussed in this chapter, and writing is discussed in Chapter 3. The examples come from Leah's essay, "Razor Wire Sweat Lodge."

PREWRITING

Freewriting

One prewriting strategy is **freewriting**, an exercise that its originator, Peter Elbow, has called "babbling in print." In freewriting, you write without stopping, letting your ideas tumble forth. You do not concern yourself with the fundamentals of writing, such as punctuation and spelling. Freewriting is an adventure into your memory and imagination. It is discovery, invention, and exploration. If you are at a loss for words on your subject, write down a comment such as "I don't know what is coming next" or "blah, blah, blah," and continue when relevant words come. The important thing is not to stop writing. Freewriting immediately eliminates the blank page and thereby helps you break through an emotional barrier, but that is not the only benefit. The words that you sort through in that idea kit will include some you can use. You can then underline or circle those words and even add notes on the side so that the freewriting continues to grow even after its initial, spontaneous expression.

The way you proceed depends on the type of assignment:

> working with a topic of your choice
> working from a restricted list of topics
> working with a prescribed topic

The *topic of your choice* gives you the greatest freedom of exploration. You would probably select a subject that interests you and freewrite about it. You allow your mind to wander among its many parts, perhaps mixing fact and fantasy, direct experience, and hearsay. A freewriting about music might uncover areas of special interest and knowledge, such as jazz or folk rock, that you would want to pursue further in freewriting or other prewriting strategies.

Working from a *restricted list* requires a more focused kind of freewriting. With the list, you can, of course, experiment with several topics to discover what is most suitable for you. If, for example, "career choice," "career preparation," "career guidance," and "career prospects" are on the restricted list, you would probably select one and freewrite about that. If it works well for you, you would probably proceed with the next step of your prewriting. If you are not satisfied with what you uncover in freewriting, you would explore another item from the restricted list.

When working with a *prescribed topic,* you focus on a particular topic and try to restrict your freewriting to its boundaries. If your topic specifies a division of a subject area such as "political involvement of your generation," then you would tie those key words to your own information, critical thinking, and imaginative responses. If the topic is restricted to, let's say, a particular reading selection such as your reactions to a poem, then that poem would give you a framework for freewriting about your own experiences, creations, and opinions. An analysis of the piece would probably include underlining pertinent ideas, annotating it (writing in the margins), and even taking notes on it. Freewriting can help you get words on paper to generate topics, develop new insights, and explore ideas.

Freewriting can lead to other stages of prewriting and writing, and it can also provide content for details and insights as you develop your topic. Let's back up and see how Leah used freewriting to begin exploring her ideas for her essay. Leah was assigned to write a personal essay of 500 to 800 words. Her instructor suggested she concentrate on a recent development or prison event that changed her life, for better or worse.

Several topics interested her. There was the problem of overcrowding: she lived in an institution built for 900 inmates, and the population was now 2,200. She also considered education. After spending some time in routine prison work and aimless activities, she had discovered school and found it highly satisfying. And then there were the accomplishments of her Native American friends at the prison. After years of arguing their case, they had finally obtained permission from the institution to build a sweat lodge for religious purposes, and it was now in operation. That was a subject she knew well, and it was one for which she held the most enthusiasm.

Leah started freewriting, which enabled her to probe her memory and see which aspects of the subject she was most interested in. She wrote without stopping, letting her ideas tumble forth in order to liberate and associate the many thoughts she had on the subject of "sweat lodge." Following is some of Leah's freewriting.

> For several years I have wanted to
> worship in the way that I did when I was on
> the reservation. These people here at prison
> were discriminating against me, I thought. I

knew that the other people here could go to
the chaplain and to the chapel and they could
do so without people complaining or going to
any bother. I didn't know why they did not
allow me to follow my own religious
preference. Then I talked to the other Indian
sisters here at prison and they told me that
they had been working for many years to get a
sweat lodge. I started working with them. It
took years of work, but it is worth it for

Have sweat lodge now

now we have a sweat lodge where we can go for
our ceremonies. It makes me feel good. I look
forward to it. I have used it once a week for
most of the last year. When I am nervous and
when things are tense on the prison grounds,
I think about the sweat lodge and just
thinking about it gives me some peace. Then
when I go there and sweat for a period of
time I seem to feel that I am leaving the
prison grounds and I am at peace with the

Ceremony important

universe. It is a ceremony that is important
to me and also to the prison. We even have
women who are not Indians who are interested
and we teach them about Indian ways and we
all learn from what we do. What else is there
to say. I could go on and on. That is what I
have to say. I love the sweat lodge which we
call the sweats. I think it is the most

> important thing in my life now. I used to be
>
> bitter toward the prison for denying me my
>
> **At peace**   rights, but now I am even <u>at peace</u> with them—
>
> most of the time. I remember when we were
>
> trying to get approval and . . . [partial]

After her freewriting session, Leah examined what she had written for possible ideas to develop for a writing assignment. As she recognized those ideas, she underlined key words and phrases and made a few notes in the margins. By reading only the underlined words above, you can understand what is important to Leah; it was not necessary for her to underline whole sentences.

In addition to putting words on that dreaded blank sheet of paper, Leah discovered that she had quite a lot to say about the sweat lodge and that she had selected a favorable topic to develop. The entire process took no more than five minutes. Had she found only a few ideas or no promising ideas at all, she might have freewritten on another topic. In going back over her work she saw some errors, especially in wording and sentence structure, but she did not correct them because the purpose of freewriting is discovery, not revising or correcting grammar, punctuation, and spelling. She was confident that she could continue with the process of writing a paper.

▌ EXERCISE 1

Freewrite for a few minutes on one of the following topics. After you finish freewriting, take two minutes or so to mark the key words and phrases. Then make a few notations if you find some promising ideas that could be developed.

> An event that was important to you in your youth
> A concert, a movie, or a television program
> Types of radio stations
> Drugs—causes, effects, a friend with a problem
> Gangs—causes, effects, an experience
> Ways of disciplining children
> A family reunion, wedding, funeral, or graduation
> A great or terrible party

A bad or good day at school
Why a college education is important
How music (rock, rap, country) affects or reveals the attitudes
    of its fans
Your most memorable job
A date from hell or heaven

Brainstorming and Listing

Brainstorming is a strategy for coming up with fresh, new ideas
in a hurry. What key words and phrases pop into your mind when
you think about your topic? One effective way to get started
brainstorming is to ask the "big six questions" about your subject
area: Who? What? Where? When? Why? and How? Then let your
mind run free as you jot down answers in single entries or lists.
Using the big six questions also helps you begin to organize ideas
for your writing. Some of the big six questions may not fit, and
some may be more important than others, depending on the purpose of your writing. For example, if you were writing about the
causes of an accident, the Why? question could be more important than the others. If you were concerned with how to succeed
in college, the How? question would predominate. If you were
writing in response to a reading selection, you would confine
your thinking to questions related to the content of the reading
selection.

    Whatever the focus of the six questions, the result is likely to
be numerous ideas that will provide information for continued exploration and development of your topic. Thus your pool of information for writing widens and deepens.

    An alternative to the big six questions approach is simply to
make a list of words and phrases related to your subject area or specific topic.

    Leah continued with the subject of bad drivers, and her topic
tightened to focus on particular areas. Although she could have
listed the annotations and the words she underlined in her freewriting, she instead used the big six questions for her framework.

Who?   American Indian inmates and others
What?   sweat lodge—how it was started—the politics—the
              ceremonies

Where?   California Institution for Women—off the yard
When?   1989, before, after, long time in planning and build-
          ing
Why?   spiritual, physical, self-esteem, educational
How?   preparation, steps

Leah's listing might have taken this form:

Sweat lodge	Ceremony	Result
Problems in building it	Preparation	Relaxed
Reasons	Blankets	Spiritually clean
Fairness	Rocks	Peaceful
Who helped	Fire	
Time to build	Water	
	Tobacco and sweet grass	
	Sweating	
	Passing pipe	
	Tearing down	

<hr>

EXERCISE 2

Brainstorm or make a list for the topic that interested you in
Exercise 1.

Clustering

Still another prewriting technique is *clustering* (also called *map-
ping*). Start by "double-bubbling" your topic. That is, write it down
in the middle of the page and draw a double circle around it, like
the hub of a wheel. Then, respond to the question, What comes to
mind? Single-bubble other ideas on spokes radiating from the hub.
Any bubble can lead to another bubble or to numerous bubbles in
the same way. This strategy is sometimes used instead of or before
making an outline to organize and develop ideas.

The more specific the topic inside the double bubble, the fewer
the spokes that will radiate from it. For example, a topic such as
"high school dropouts" would have more spokes than "reasons for
dropping out of high school."

Here is Leah's cluster on her topic of the prison sweat lodge.

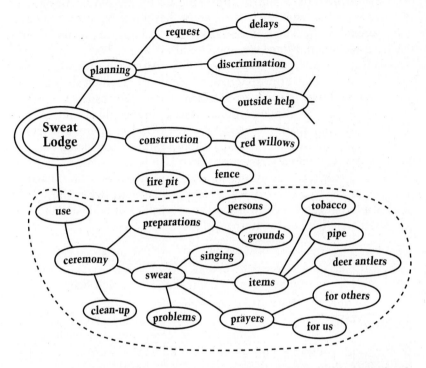

Notice that after completing her basic cluster, Leah went back and drew a broken boundary around subclusters that offered encouraging areas for focus. Some subclusters, usually with further clustering to provide details, can be as good as an outline in offering structure and content for the development of an essay.

EXERCISE 3

Using a clean sheet of paper, make a cluster on the topic you have chosen. After you finish, draw broken boundaries around subclusters that have potential for further writing.

Composing the Thesis

After freewriting, brainstorming, and clustering, Leah was ready to focus. She was ready to concentrate on one aspect of her larger topic that could reasonably be developed in an essay of 500 to 800 words. She also wanted to establish a direction for the essay that would target her audience, who knew little about her topic. It would be necessary to explain her topic in detail so that uninformed readers could easily understand. Moreover, she would avoid any Native American words that her audience might not know. Although the sweat lodge was developed in an atmosphere of controversy in which she and others often had to be persuasive, she anticipated that readers of this essay would be open-minded and interested. She would simply inform them about her experience with the sweat lodge, giving a personal perspective. She would also have to avoid using prison slang, because this essay was for an assignment in a college writing class.

Leah made three attempts to write a sentence with both a subject (what she would write about) and a treatment (what she would do with her subject). She wanted the treatment to be just right, not vague or too broad or too narrow.

> I want to explain how we use the sweats and why.
>
> Using the prison sweat lodge involves specific practices that contribute to my well-being.
>
> Subject   I want to discuss the <u>prison sweat lodge,</u> <u>what we</u>
> Treatment <u>do in the preparation period,</u> <u>what we do when</u>
> <u>we're inside for the ceremony, and what we do</u>
> <u>afterwards.</u>

Her third attempt satisfied her, and the statement became her thesis. Later she would reword it.

▎ EXERCISE 4

After consulting your freewriting, brainstorming or listing, and clustering, write a thesis. Label the subject and treatment parts.

Outlining

Outlining is the tool that most people think of in connection with organizing. Outlining does basically the same thing that listing and clustering do. *Outlining divides the controlling idea into sections of support material, divides those sections further, and establishes sequence.*

An outline is a kind of framework, and it can be used in two ways. It can indicate the plan for a paragraph or essay you intend to write. It can also show the organization of a passage you are reading.

The outline of a reading passage and the outline as a plan for writing are identical in form. If you intend to write a summary of a reading selection, then a single outline might be used for both purposes.

The two main outline forms are the *sentence outline* (each entry is a complete sentence) and the *topic outline* (each entry is a key word or phrase). The topic outline is more common in writing paragraphs and essays.

In the following topic outline, notice first how the parts are arranged on the page: the indentations, the number and letter sequences, the punctuation, and the placement of words. Then read the outline and see how the ideas relate to one another.

Main idea (usually the topic sentence for a paragraph or the thesis for an essay)

I. Major support
  A. Minor support
    1. Explanation, detail, example
    2. Explanation, detail, example
  B. Minor support
    1. Explanation, detail, example
    2. Explanation, detail, example
II. Major support
  A. Minor support
    1. Explanation, detail, example
    2. Explanation, detail, example
  B. Minor support
    1. Explanation, detail, example
    2. Explanation, detail, example

Leah's next task was to organize her material. For this strategy, she went back to her bubble cluster, which she had divided into "planning," "construction," and "use." She had already decided she wanted to work with the "use" aspect and explain it from her perspective. Therefore, she focused on only one part of the cluster—the part indicated by the broken boundary line.

She might have started to write a first draft at this point, but instead she decided she wanted to recall and organize more detail, so she began an outline. She used her own memory and private reference sources for information. If she had been working on a reading-related topic, she would have gone back to the reading. If she had been working on a topic subject to research, she would have consulted library sources.

The outline shows the relationship of ideas, suggests ways to divide the essay according to Leah's thesis, and indicates support. The divisions are Preparation, Ceremony, and Ceremony completion and Site restoration. Those items are Leah's Roman numeral headings.

    I. Preparation
        A. Fasting
            1. Duration
            2. Only water
        B. Heat rocks
            1. Thirty to fifty
            2. Build fire
        C. Set up lodge
            1. Permission from sponsor
            2. Cover framework
   II. Ceremony
        A. Movement
            1. Going and coming
            2. Passing sacred objects
        B. Establishing attitude
        C. Sweating
        D. Praying and singing
        E. Purification rites
            1. Tobacco ties
            2. Sage
            3. Sweet grass
  III. Ceremony completion and site restoration
        A. Personal
            1. Water down
            2. Eat and drink
            3. Change
        B. Site
            1. Remove and store blankets
            2. Move rocks

| EXERCISE 5 |

Fill in the missing parts of the following outlines. It may be helpful to consider, in each case, whether you are dealing with time, examples, causes, effects, parts, or steps. The answers will vary, depending on your individual experiences and views.

1. Borrowing   is the mother of trouble.
       subject   treatment

    I. Receive five credit cards in mail

   II. Saw numerous commercials on television

      A. One about _____

      B. Another about _____

  III. Made purchases

  IV. Two months later _____

2. A successful job interview   depends on several factors.
              subject   treatment

    I. Good appearance

      A. _____

      B. _____

   II. Behaving properly

  III. Being qualified

      A. Education

      B. _____

  IV. Knowing something about the employer

3. Joe's drug addiction   had significant effects on his life.
         subject   treatment

    I. Developed mental health problems

      A. _____

      B. _____

   II. Developed _____

  III. Lost his job

EXERCISE 6

For this final technique of prewriting, make a topic outline for your essay. Your Roman numeral headings will probably correspond with some of the major divisions of your cluster.

Writer's Guidelines at a Glance:
The Writing Process—Prewriting

1. The writing process consists of strategies that can help you pro-
   duce a polished essay. *Prewriting* includes exploring, experimenting, gathering information, writing the controlling idea,
   and organizing and developing support. *Writing* includes drafting, revising, and editing.

2. Prewriting includes one or more of the following strategies.

   > *Freewriting:* writing without stopping so that you can ex-
   > plore, experiment, and invent
   >
   > *Brainstorming or listing:* responding to *Who? What? Where?
   > When? Why? How?* questions or making lists on likely di-
   > visions of your subject
   >
   > *Clustering:* showing related ideas by "double-bubbling" a
   > subject and then connecting single bubbles of related ideas
   > on spokes radiating out and branching from the hub
   >
   > *Composing the thesis:* writing a sentence that has two
   > parts—the subject (what you are writing about) and th
   > treatment (what you will do with the subject
   >
   > *Outlining:* dividing the controlling idea into sections of sup-
   > port material, dividing those sections further, and estab-
   > lishing a workable sequence

3

The Writing Process: Writing, Revising, and Editing

WRITING YOUR FIRST DRAFT

Once you have developed your thesis and your outline (or list or cluster), you are ready to begin writing your essay. The initial writing is called the first, or rough, draft. Your thesis statement is likely to be at or near the beginning of your essay and will be followed by your support as ordered by your outline.

Paying close attention to your outline for basic organization, you should proceed without worrying about the refinements of writing. This is not the time to concern yourself with perfect spelling, grammar, or punctuation. After you have finished that first draft, take a close look at it. If your thesis is sound and your outline has served you well, you now have a basic discussion. You have made a statement and supported it.

Don't be embarrassed by the roughness of your work. You should be embarrassed only if you leave it that way. You are seeing the reason why a first draft is called "rough." Famous authors have said publicly that they wouldn't show their rough drafts even to their closest, most forgiving friends.

The Recursive Factor

The process of writing can be called recursive, which means "going back and forth." In this respect, writing is like reading. If you do not understand what you have read, you back up and read it again. After you have read an entire passage, you may need to read it again selectively. The same can be said of writing. If, for example, after having developed an outline and started writing your first draft, you

29

discover that your subject is too broad, you will have to back up, narrow your thesis, and then adjust your outline. You may even want to return to an early cluster of ideas to see how you can use a smaller grouping of them. Revision is usually the most recursive of all parts of the writing process. You will go over your material again and again until you are satisfied that you have expressed yourself as well as you possible can.

Your Audience

When you speak to a person, you routinely adjust what you say and how you say it. You should do the same for your audience when you write. To the extent that you can, consider the needs, interests, knowledge, and abilities of your intended readers and appropriately adjust your subject, explanations, style, and word choice.

REVISING YOUR WRITING

The term *first draft* suggests quite accurately that there will be other drafts, or versions, of your writing. Only in the most dire situations, such as an in-class examination when you have time for only one draft, should you be satisfied with a single effort.

What you do beyond the first draft is revising and editing. Revising concerns itself with organization, content, and language effectiveness. Editing involves correcting in spelling, punctuation, and capitalization. In practice, revising and editing are not always separate activities, though writers usually wait until the next-to-the-last draft to edit some minor details and attend to other small points that can be easily overlooked.

Successful revision almost always involves intense, systematic rewriting. You should learn to look for certain aspects of skillful writing as you enrich and repair your first draft. To help you recall these aspects so that you can keep them in mind and examine your material in a comprehensive fashion, this textbook offers a memory device—an acronym in which each letter suggests an important feature of good writing and revision. This device enables you to memorize the features of good writing quickly. Soon you will be able to recall and refer to them automatically. These features need not be attended to individually when you revise your writing, though they may be. And they need not be attended to in the order presented here. The acronym is CLUESS (pronounced "clues"), which provides this guide:

Coherence
Language
Unity
Emphasis
Support
Sentences

Coherence

Coherence is an orderly relationship of ideas, each leading smoothly and logically to the next. You must weave your ideas together so skillfully that the reader can easily see how one idea connects to another and to the central thought. This central thought, of course, is expressed in the topic sentence for a paragraph and in the thesis for an essay. You can achieve coherence efficiently by using an overall pattern, transitional words and expressions, repetition of key words and ideas, pronouns, and a consistent point of view.

Overall Pattern

Several chapters in this book discuss strategies for an overall plan, or pattern of organization. Three basic patterns prevail: *time* (chronology), *space*, and *emphasis* (stress on ideas). Sometimes you will combine patterns. The coherence of each can be strengthened by using transitional words such as these:

> For a time pattern: *first, then, soon, later, following, after, at that point*
> For a space pattern: *up, down, right, left, beyond, behind, above, below, before*
> For an emphasis pattern: *first, second, third, most, more*

Transitional Terms

By using transitional terms, conjunctive adverbs, you can help your readers move easily from one idea to another. Each of the sentences below has one or more of these terms.

Others include *moreover, in fact, nevertheless, then, thus, now, soon, therefore, consequently,* and *accordingly.*

> *First* I realized I had to get a job to stay in school.
> *At the same time, however,* my track coach wanted the team to spend more hours working out.
> We were, *after all,* the defending champions.
> *Finally* I dropped one of my courses.

Repetition of Key Words and Ideas

Repeat key words and phrases to keep the main subject in the reader's mind and to maintain the continuity necessary for a smooth flow of logical thought.

Pronouns

Pronouns, such as *this, that, those, he, her, them,* and *it,* provide natural connecting links in your writing. Why? Every pronoun refers to an earlier noun (called the *antecedent* of the pronoun) and thus carries the reader back to that earlier thought. Here are some examples:

> I tried to buy *tickets* for the concert, but *they* were all sold.

> Assertive *people* tend to make decisions quickly. However, *they* may not make the wisest decisions.

Language

In the revision process, the word *language* takes on a special meaning; it refers to usage, tone, and diction.

Usage

Usage is the kind or general style of language we use. All or almost all of us operate on the principle of appropriateness. If I used *ain't* as part of my explanations in this textbook, you would be surprised and probably disappointed. You would think about my word choice rather than what I have to say. Why would you be surprised? Because *ain't* is not appropriate for my audience in this situation. If you write an essay containing slang, you will probably be understood, but if the slang is not appropriate, you will draw unfavorable attention to your words. That does not mean that slang does not have its place—it does. It can be imaginative and colorful. Often, though, it is only a weak substitute for a more precise vocabulary.

Usage is an important part of writing and revising. Judge what is appropriate for your audience and your purpose. What kind of language is expected? What kind of language is best suited for accomplishing your purpose?

Tone

Have you ever heard someone say, "Don't talk to me in that tone of voice" or "I accepted what she was saying, but I didn't like the tone she used when she told me"? *Tone* in these contexts means that the sound of the speaker's voice and maybe the language choices conveyed disrespect to the listener. The tone could have represented any number of feelings about the subject matter and the audience. Tone can have as many variations as you can have feelings: it can, for example, be sarcastic, humorous, serious, cautionary, objective, groveling, angry, bitter, sentimental, enthusiastic, somber, outraged, or loving.

Let's say you are getting a haircut. Looking in those omnipresent mirrors bordered with pictures of people with different styles of haircuts, you see that the barber is cutting off too much hair. You could use different tones in giving him or her some timely how-to instructions.

> Objective, serious: "If you don't mind, what I meant to say was that I would like a haircut proportioned just like that one there in the picture of Tom Cruise from *Rain Man.*"
>
> Humorous: "I hesitate to make suggestions to someone who is standing at my back and holding a sharp instrument near my throat, but I'm letting my hair grow out a bit, and I don't want you to take off a lot in the back and on the sides."
>
> Angry and sarcastic: "Look man, when I sat down, I said I wanted my hair cut in the design of Tom Cruise in *Rain Man.* The way you're hacking at it, you must've thought I said *Top Gun.*"
>
> Conciliatory: "I really like the way you cut my hair, and I can see that you are proportioning it with great care, but I would like my hair to be a bit longer than the style that I think you're working on. Do you remember how I used to get my hair cut about a year ago, a little longer on the sides and more bushy on top?"
>
> Friendly: "You came up with a great style that everyone liked. Could you give me one similar to that?"
>
> Overbearing: "Damn it, buddy. Will you watch what you're doing! I asked for a haircut, not a shave. If God had wanted me to have bare skin above my shoulders, he would've put the hair on my feet."

In speech, feelings and attitudes are represented by inflection, loudness, word choice, and language patterns. In writing, tone is conveyed mainly by word choice and order; it is closely related to style—the variations in the way you write, depending on your purpose. Your purpose is simply to present a particular idea in a particular context. The context implies the audience; it is important to use the tone appropriate for your audience.

Usually your tone will be consistent throughout your presentation, although for the informal essay often assigned in college, you may choose to begin in a light-hearted, amusing tone before switching to a more serious, objective mode.

Diction

Diction is word choice. If you use good diction, you are finding the best words for a particular purpose in addressing a certain audience. There is some overlap, therefore, between usage and diction.

Here is a chart showing the difference between general and specific words.

General	Specific	More Specific
food	hamburger	Hefty Burger
mess	grease	oil slicks on table
drink	soda	mug of root beer
odor	smell from grill	smell of frying onions

Another aspect of diction is freshness and originality of expression. To achieve those distinctions, you should avoid clichés, which are trite, familiar phrases. Consider this sentence:

> When the prince married Cinderella, her sisters went green with envy because she was now on easy street, leaving them out in the cold.

Those words were written by a person who doesn't care about communicating in a clear and interesting manner. It would be far better to say,

> When the prince married Cinderella, her sisters were envious because they had few prospects.

Here is a list of some clichés to avoid:

young at heart	quick as a flash
rotten to the core	slow but sure
uphill battle	other side of the coin
more than meets the eye	breathless silence
bitter end	acid test
as luck would have it	better late than never
last but not least	six of one, half dozen of the other

These are ready-made expressions. A cliché master manipulates language as if it were a prefabricated building going up, not bothering to use any imagination and leaving little opportunity for his or her audience to use theirs. Good diction, on the other hand, reflects the writer as an individual and is fresh, original, and clear.

Unity

A controlling idea, stated or implied, unifies every piece of good writing. It is the point around which the supporting material revolves. For a paragraph, the elements are the topic sentence and the supporting sentences. For the essay, the elements are the thesis and the supporting paragraphs. All the supporting material should be related to the topic sentence or thesis.

Unity can be strengthened and made more apparent if you use a strong concluding statement at the end of the unit and if you repeat key words and phrases from time to time. A good check on unity is to ask yourself if everything in your paragraph or essay is subordinate to and derived from the controlling idea.

Don't confuse unity and coherence. Whereas coherence involves the clear movement of thought from sentence to sentence or paragraph to paragraph, unity means staying on the topic. A unified and coherent outline would become incoherent if the parts were scrambled, but the outline technically would still be unified. The point to remember is that these qualities of writing go together. You should stay on the topic and make clear connections.

Emphasis

Emphasis, a feature of most good writing, helps the reader focus on the main ideas. It can be achieved in several ways but mainly through placement of key ideas and through repetition.

Placement of Ideas

The most emphatic part of any passage, whether a sentence or a book, is the last part, because we usually remember most easily what we read last. The second most emphatic part of a passage is the beginning, because our mind is relatively uncluttered when we read it. For these reasons, among others, the topic sentence or thesis is usually at the beginning of a piece, and it is often restated or reflected on at the end in an echoing statement.

Repetition of Key Words and Ideas

Repetition is one of the simplest devices in your writer's toolbox. The words repeated may be single words, phrases, slightly altered sentences, or synonyms. Repetition keeps the dominant subject in the reader's mind and maintains the continuity necessary for a smooth flow of logical thought.

You can use this valuable technique easily. If, as is done in the following example, you are discussing the effects of school dropout, then the words *effect(s)*, along with synonyms such as *result(s)* or *consequence(s)*, and *school dropout(s)* are likely to be repeated several times. Moreover, phrases giving insight into the issue may be repeated, perhaps with slight variation.

> The causes of the school <u>dropout</u> problem have received much attention recently, but the <u>effects</u> are just as important. One obvious <u>result</u> is that of unemployment or low-paying employment. The student who <u>drops out</u> of school is likely to be <u>dropping</u> into poverty, perhaps even into a lifelong condition. Another <u>effect</u> is juvenile crime. The young person who has no prospects for a good job and no hope all too frequently turns to illegal activities. A third <u>result</u> concerns the psychological well-being of the dropout. Although <u>withdrawing</u> from school seems to offer a quick, viable solution to perceived problems, it almost immediately has <u>consequences</u> for the <u>dropout</u>'s self-esteem. Of course, these <u>effects</u> may also be tied to causes, such as drugs, poverty, crime, or psychological problems, but devastating <u>repercussions</u> are there at the far end of the causes-and-effects continuum, and youngsters who are contemplating <u>dropping</u> out should consider them with care.

A word of warning: The effective use of word and phrase repetition should not be confused with an irritating misuse of word repetition. We all at times get "hung up" on certain words, and the result is a negative response from our audience. Consider this awkward use of repetition:

> She looked at him and frowned. He returned the look and then looked away at a stranger looking for his lost keys.

That's too many *look's*. Consider this version:

> She looked at him (or, *perhaps even better,* She frowned at him). He glared back and then glanced away at a stranger searching for his lost keys.

The second version preserves the idea of people "looking" by using synonyms. It does not grate on the reader's mind as the first does.

Support

How much support does a piece of writing need? A good support paragraph fulfills its function by fully developing the topic sentence. An essay is complete when it fulfills its function of developing a thesis. Obviously, you will have to judge what is complete. With some subjects, you will need little supporting and explanatory material. With others, you will need much more. Incompleteness, not overdevelopment, is more common among beginning writers. Besides having enough support, be sure that the points of support are presented in the best possible sequence.

Consider the following paragraph. Is it complete? Does the writer make the main idea clear and provide adequate support for it? Are the ideas in the right order?

> A cat's tail is a good barometer of its intentions. By various movements of its tail a cat will signal many of its wants. Other movements indicate its attitudes. An excited or aggressively aroused cat will whip its entire tail back and forth.

At first glance, this paragraph seems complete. It begins with a concise topic sentence telling us that a cat's tail is a good barometer of its intentions. It adds information of a general nature in the following two sentences. Then it presents a supporting example about the aggressively aroused cat. But the paragraph is not explicit; there is insufficient supporting material for the opening generalization. The paragraph leaves the reader with too much information to fill in. What are some other ways that cats communicate their intentions with their tails? How do they communicate specific wishes or desires? Is their communication effective? If the passage is to answer these questions that may come into the reader's mind, it must present more material to support the beginning generalization. The original paragraph that follows begins with a concise topic sentence that is then supported with particulars.

> A cat's tail is a good barometer of its intentions. An excited or aggressively aroused cat will whip its entire tail back and forth. When I talk to Sam, he holds up his end of the conversation by occasionally flicking the tip of his tail. Mother cats move their tails back and forth to invite their kittens to play. A kitten raises its tail perpendicularly to beg for attention; older cats may do so to beg for food. When your cat holds its tail aloft while crisscrossing in front of you, it is trying to say, "Follow me"—usually to the kitchen, or more precisely, to the refrigerator. Unfortunately, many cats have lost their tails in refrigerator doors as a consequence.

Michael W. Fox, "What is Your Pet Trying to Tell You?"

We can strengthen our understanding of good support by analyzing the structure of our model paragraph, putting to use the information we have assimilated to this point in the discussion. The paragraph begins with the highest generalization (the main idea in the topic sentence): "A cat's tail is a good barometer of its intentions." It follows immediately with six major supporting statements and ends with a final sentence to add humor to the writing. If we place this material in outline form, we can easily see the recurrent pattern in the flow of thought from general to particular.

TOPIC SENTENCE (HIGHEST GENERALIZATION)	A cat's tail is a good barometer of its intentions.
MAJOR SUPPORT	A. An excited or aggressively aroused cat will whip its entire tail back and forth.
MAJOR SUPPORT	B. When I talk to Sam, he holds up his end of the conversation by occasionally flicking the tip of his tail.
MAJOR SUPPORT	C. Mother cats move their tails back and forth to invite their kittens to play.
MAJOR SUPPORT	D. A kitten raises its tail perpendicularly to beg for attention;
MAJOR SUPPORT	E. older cats may do so to beg for food.
MAJOR SUPPORT	F. When your cat holds its tail aloft while crisscrossing in front of you, it is trying to say, "Follow me"—usually to the kitchen, or more precisely, to the refrigerator.
CONCLUDING SENTENCE (ADDED FOR HUMOR)	Unfortunately, many cats have lost their tails in refrigerator doors as a consequence.

Sentences

In the revision process, the term *sentences* pertains to the variety of sentence patterns and the correctness of sentence structure.

Variety of Sentences

A passage that offers a variety of simple and complicated sentences satisfies the reader, just as a combination of simple and complicated foods go together in a good meal. The writer can introduce variety by including both short and long sentences, by using different sentence patterns, and by beginning sentences in different ways.

Length

In revising, examine your writing to make sure that sentences vary in length. A series of short sentences is likely to make the flow seem choppy and the thoughts disconnected. But single short sentences often work very well. Because they are uncluttered with supporting points and qualifications, they are often direct and forceful. Consider using short sentences to emphasize points and to introduce ideas. Use longer sentences to provide details or show how ideas are related.

Variety of Sentence Patterns

Good writing includes a variety of sentence patterns. Although there is no limit to the number of sentences you can write, the conventional English sentence appears in only four basic patterns:

Simple	She did the work well.
Compound	She did the work well, and she was well paid.
Complex	Because she did the work well, she was well paid.
Compound-complex	Because she did the work well, she was well paid, and she was satisfied.

Each sentence pattern listed above has its own purposes and strengths. The simple sentence conveys a single idea. The compound sentence shows, by its structure, that two somewhat equal ideas are connected. The complex sentence shows that one idea is less important than another; that is, it is dependent on, or subordinate to, the idea in the main clause. The compound-complex sentence has the scope of both the compound sentence and the complex sentence.

Variety of Sentence Beginnings

Another way to provide sentence variety is to use different kinds of beginnings. A new beginning may or may not be accompanied by a changed sentence pattern. Among the most common beginnings, other than those starting with the subject of the main clause, are those that start with a prepositional phrase, a dependent clause, or a transitional connective (conjunctive adverb), such as *therefore, however,* or *in fact.*

- Prepositional phrase (in italics)

  In your fantasy, you are the star.
  Like casino owners, game show hosts want you to be cheery.

- Dependent clause (in italics)

  When the nighttime Wheel of Fortune *debuted,* the slot was occupied by magazine shows.
  As Pat Sajak noted, viewers often solve the puzzle before the contestants do.

  (Examples from "A Big Wheel," Lewis Grossberger)

- Transitional connective (in italics)

  Now you know.
  Therefore, you feel happy, excited, and a bit superior.

Problems with Sentences

A complete sentence must generally include an independent clause, which is a group of words that contain a subject and a verb and can stand alone. Some groups of words may sound interesting, but they are not correct sentences. Three common problem groupings are the fragment, the comma splice, and the run-on (see Handbook page 195).

- *Fragment:* A word grouping that is structurally incomplete is only a fragment of a sentence.

  Because he left.
  (This is a dependent clause, not a complete sentence.)
  Went to the library.
  (This one has no subject.)
  She being the only person there.
  (This has no verb.)
  Waiting there for help.
  (This phrase has neither subject nor verb.)
  In the back seat under a book.
  (Here we have two prepositional phrases but no subject or verb.)

- *Comma splice:* The comma splice consists of two independent clauses with only a comma between them.

The weather was bad, we canceled the picnic.
(A comma by itself cannot join two independent clauses.)

- *Run-on:* The run-on differs from the comma splice in only one way: it has no comma between the independent clauses.

The weather was bad we canceled the picnic.

Fragments, comma splices, and run-ons can easily be fixed. You cannot fix them, however, until you can confidently identify them in your writing. Watch out for them during the revision and editing stages of your writing.

If you frequently have problems with sentence structure and awkwardness of phrasing, be especially suspicious of long sentences. Test each sentence of fifteen or more words for flaws. Try writing shorter, more direct sentences until you gain more confidence and competency. Then work with more sophisticated patterns.

Editing Your Writing

This final stage of the writing process involves a careful examination of your work. Look for problems with capitalization, omissions, punctuation, and spelling. (COPS).

Before you submit your writing to your instructor, do what almost all professional writers do before sending their material along: read it aloud, to yourself or to a willing accomplice. Reading material aloud will help you catch awkwardness of expression, omission and misplacement of words, and other problems that are easily overlooked by an author.

As you can see, writing is a process and is not a matter of just sitting down and "banging out" a statement. The parts of the process from prewriting to revising to editing are connected, and your movement is ultimately forward, but this process allows you to go back and forth in the recursive manner discussed earlier. If your outline is not working, perhaps the flaw is in your thesis. You may need to go back and fix it. If one section of your essay is skimpy, perhaps you will have to go back and reconsider the pertinent material in your outline or clustering. There you might find more details or alter your thesis so that you can move into more fertile areas of thought.

Let's return to Leah, whose work was shown in Chapters 1 and 2. After completing her first draft, she began revising, guided mainly by CLUESS:

<u>C</u>oherence	one idea leading smoothly to the next
<u>L</u>anguage	usage, tone, and diction
<u>U</u>nity	using the thesis to unify the essay parts and the topic sentences to unify the developmental paragraphs
<u>E</u>mphasis	repetition of words and phrases and placement of key parts at the beginning or end of units
<u>S</u>upport	presenting evidence and reasoning in relation to the thesis and topic sentences
<u>S</u>entences	using a variety of beginnings and patterns; avoiding fragments, comma splices, and run-ons

The following draft is not her first nor her last, but it is an early draft that shows her revision process. The draft also includes some editing (for *c*apitalization, *o*missions, *p*unctuation, and *s*pelling, or COPS).

Razor Wire Sweat Lodge

               My tribe is   twenty-one represented
~~I am a~~ Pomo ~~Indian,~~ one ~~tribe~~ of ~~many~~
                      always
~~here~~ on the prison grounds. I have had

                        Ancestors   in

Rewrite:

tremendous interest in my ~~Ancestry~~ and their

customs, and the cultures of all Indian

tribes. The sacred sweat ceremonies, I've
                       cultural practices
found to be one of the most interesting. Many
   other
women of ~~all~~ races here in the facility have
                 other benefits
also taken interest and found ~~peace~~ within

themselves from participating in the sweats.

I want to discuss the prison sweat lodge,

what we do in the preparation period, what we

do when we're inside for the ceremony, and

what we do afterwards.

Rewrite for
stronger topic
sentence [

The first step to sweating ^(in our prison facility) is the

preparation period. Before anyone can sweat

there are many requirements ^~~in~~ concerning what we wear /

~~how we are instructed (depending on how many~~

~~times we've gone),~~ and how we act. ^(For) ~~T~~wenty-

four hours before the sweat ^(Participants should drink only) we fast. ~~We can~~

Coherence [

~~only drink~~ water or juices, but if someone

has health problems, we will excuse her. The

lava rocks have to ^(heat) in the fire approximately

three hours before we start sweating. The

Organize
Be more
concise [

fire has to be built just right in a little

house shape. ~~Putting~~ ^(We put) all the rocks in the

middle with the wood standing like a teepee

around them; then the paper ^(is) stuffed between

and around the wood. Once there's a good fire

going ^, we ~~start~~ tend to the sweat lodge

itself. Since we have no tarp to put on the

sweat lodge, the state has provided us with

plenty of blankets. The blankets have to cover

the s(w)eat lodge fully. We put at least three

layers of blankets on the sweat lodge. We make

sure we leave about eight inches of blanket

around the bottom of the sweat lodge. ~~Around~~ By

Coherence [this time some women have started making their

tobacco ties. These ties are used for ~~putting~~ sending

~~your~~ prayer on. We~~'ve got to~~ must make sure the

sponsor is somewhere by the sweat lodge at all

times. ~~Also about~~ As for the rock(s,) we use thirty to

fifty of them(,) it depends on their size and how

many women are sweating that day. Then the

women are told to change into only muumuu(s); the

state provides them also. Then we're read(y) to go

inside. The preparation period is very

important ~~and~~ but everyone looks forward to it

being over.

Once everyone is inside the sweat lodge,

there are certain things ~~you~~ we must do. ~~The way

we enter is~~ first we enter counter clockwise

(once) and inside we ~~maintain everything we do~~ conduct all parts of the ceremony

counter clockwise. There are four rounds in

the sweat which lasts about twenty to thirty

minutes ~~each~~. We stress that no one break our

circle inside the sweat lodge, but it ~~is~~

coherence [~~possible.~~ Some women can't handle the heat

inside we never make them stay. The praying

Rephrase and singing is in the Sioux language since

our outside sponsor is Sioux. Not everyone

has to sing or pray. It's up to ~~them~~. As

someone finishes a prayer ~~they say for all~~

~~their relations~~, then the next person prays.

Agr [Before ~~anyone even~~ enters the sweat ~~they~~

have to make sure they have peace and

good feelings with all other members. The

tobacco ties hang over our heads in the

sweat or around our necks. (Also) we take in

sage with us and smudge ourselves with it.

After each round, new hot rocks are brought

Verb [in. As these rocks are place in the fire
tense

sweet grass is put on them. ~~All~~ we do inside

Be more the sweat lodge is not only for ourselves,
concise

but ~~for~~ our prayers for others. We maintain

Editorial corrections shown above the line:
- each
- should
- sometimes happens.
- the individual.
- she mentions all her relatives
- we ... we
- for purification
- d
- What
- through

Be more
concise

ourselves with humility during the whole

sweat.

When the sweat is over ∧ we enter the final

phase. We come out and throw our tobacco ties

in ∧(to) the fire pit. The ∧ⁿ ~~first thing~~ we ~~do is~~ hose

ourselves down with plenty of cold water. The

refreshments are opened and someone goes after

food. Once we've eaten and changed our clothes ∧

we start taking down the sweat. The blankets

have to be taken off the same way they were

put on and folded up ∧(carefully) ~~good~~. The left-over wood

has to be put away and ~~on both~~ the blankets

and the wood ∧(must be covered) ~~we put their covers~~. Any garbage

that's been left around is thrown in ∧(to) the

dumpster. Then we lock the gate and bid our

farewells until the next weekend. After it's

move
to end

all over ∧(we) ~~you really~~ feel (physically) ~~a sense of~~,

refresh(ed)~~ness~~, and cleanliness ∧, and peacefulness.

Rewrite

∧(Using) ~~The~~ sweat lodge is a custom of most~~ly all~~

Indian tribes. Certain Indian tribes go about

it differently ~~than~~ (from) others ∧ but once they're

all inside everyone feels of one whole being.

All three of the steps I've gone through are

helpful for a successful sweat ceremony. ~~Many~~

of ~~us members~~ look forward to these

Each week we
⋀

ceremonies ~~every week~~. They help us cope

better with the prison system.

Treat the following passage by Tara Newsome as your own rough draft and revise and edit it. First consider coherence, language, unity, emphasis, support, and sentences (CLUESS). Then edit, correcting fundamentals such as capitalization, omissions, punctuation, and spelling (COPS).

Quitting School

Quitting school was not a big deal for me until I realize all the effects of quitting would bring to my life. At that time I didn't care. I plan to marry a few months later after my high school graduation. I was happy at the time.

Quitting school was a big mistake because when I went out to look for a job I couldn't qualify for any of the good positions because of my lack of education. Instead I took a job as in a fast-foods place where I had no future. Then I went to work in a big company just doing simple office work. When it came time for promotions I couldn't pass the tests they gave. That was not all. As a result of quitting school later. I couldn't even help my children with their homework or buy the special things for them.

I started my family when I was not even eighteen years. The first year of my marriage was fine, then things started to fall apart. My husband had quit school too, and he didn't make much money, and as I mentioned, I didn't make much either. We argued a lot mainly over money. We couldn't get a big enough house for our family so that we could have the privacy we needed. I quit work to raise my kids and that when I really got in deep. My car was getting old and money was not enough to make big payments I had to buy another old car, which broke down all the time. I started freaking out. The fighting got worse and we had a divorce.

I was lucky that my parents decided to help me, and now I am dedicated to getting a good education. I will work hard to learn so me and my children can have a better life.

WRITER'S GUIDELINES AT A GLANCE: WRITING, REVISING, AND EDITING

1. **Writing**
   Write your first draft, paying close attention to your outline or list or cluster. Do not concern yourself with perfect spelling, grammar, or punctuation.

2. **Revising**

   Coherence
   - Are the ideas clearly related, each one to the others, and to the central idea?
   - Is there a clear pattern of organization (time, space, or emphasis)?

- Is the pattern supported by words that suggest the basis of that organization (time: *now, then, later;* space: *above, below, up, down;* emphasis: *first, second, last*)?
- Is coherence enhanced by the use of transitional terms, pronouns, repetition, and a consistent point of view?

Language

- Is the general style of language usage appropriate (properly standard and formal or informal) for the purpose of the piece and the intended audience?
- Is the tone (language use showing attitude toward material and audience) appropriate?
- Is the word choice (diction) effective? Are the words precise in conveying meaning? Are they fresh and original?

Unity

- Is the thesis and every topic sentence clear and well stated? Do they indicate both subject and treatment?
- Are all points of support clearly related to and subordinate to the topic sentence of each paragraph and to the thesis of the essay?

Emphasis

- Are ideas properly placed (especially near the beginning and end) for emphasis?
- Are important words and phrases repeated for emphasis?

Support

- Is there adequate material—such as examples, details, quotations, and explanations—to support each topic sentence and the thesis?
- Are the points of support placed in the best possible order?

Sentence Structure

- Are the sentences varied in length and beginnings?
- Are the sentences varied in pattern (simple, compound, complex, and compound-complex)?
- Are all problems with sentence structure (fragments, comma splices, run-ons) corrected?

3. Editing

- Are all problems in such areas as capitalization, omissions, punctuation, and spelling corrected?

4

Descriptive Narration: Moving Through Time and Space

A NATURAL COMBINATION OF NARRATION AND DESCRIPTION

As patterns of writing, description and narration go together like macaroni and cheese. You would almost never describe something without relating it to something else, especially to a story, or a narrative. And you would seldom narrate something (tell a story) without including some description. A narrative moves through time; a description moves mainly through space.

THE NARRATIVE PATTERN

In our everyday lives, we tell stories and invite other people to do so by asking questions such as "What happened at work today?" and "What did you do last weekend?" We are disappointed when the answer is "Nothing much." We may be equally disappointed when a person doesn't give us enough details or gives us too many and spoils the effect. After all, we are interested in people's stories and in the people who tell them. We like narratives.

What is a narrative? A narrative is an account of an incident or a series of incidents that make up a complete and significant action. A narrative can be as short as a joke, as long as a novel, or anything between, including the essay. Each narrative has five properties.

Situation

Situation is the background for the action. The situation may be described only briefly, or it may even be implied. ("To celebrate my seventeenth birthday, I went to the Department of Motor Vehicles to take my practical test for my driver's license.")

Conflict

Conflict is friction, such as a problem in the surroundings, with another person(s), or within the individual. The conflict, which is at the heart of each story, produces struggles. ("It was raining and my appointment was the last one of the day. The examiner was a serious, weary-looking man who reminded me of a bad boss I once had, and I was nervous.")

Struggle

Struggle, which need not be physical, is the manner of dealing with the conflict. The struggle adds action or engagement and generates the plot. ("After grinding on the ignition because the engine was already on, I had trouble finding the windshield wiper control. Next I forgot to signal until after I had pulled away from the curb. As we crept slowly down the rain-glazed street, the examiner told me to take the emergency brake off. All the while I listened to his pen scratching on his clipboard. 'Pull over and park,' he said solemnly.")

Outcome

Outcome is the result of the struggle. ("After I parked the car, the examiner told me to relax, and then he talked to me about school. When we continued, somehow I didn't make any errors, and I got my license.")

Meaning

Meaning is the significance of the story, which may be deeply philosophical or simple, stated or implied. ("calmness promotes calmness").

These components are present in some way in all the many forms of the narrative. They are enhanced by the use of various devices like the following:

- *Description* (the use of specific details to advance action, with images to make readers see, smell, taste, hear, and feel)

  "the *rain-glazed street*"

  "listened to his *pen scratching*"

- *Dialogue* (the exact words of the speakers, enclosed in quotation marks)

    "Pull over and park," he said solemnly.

- *Transitional words* (words, such as *after, finally, following, later, next, soon,* and *when,* that move a story forward, for narratives are usually presented in chronological order)

    "Next I forgot to"
    "After I parked the car"

Most narratives written as college assignments have an expository purpose (that is, they explain a specified idea). Often the narrative will be merely an extended example. Therefore, the meaning of the narrative is exceedingly important and should be clear, whether it is stated or implied.

THE DESCRIPTIVE PATTERN

Description is the use of words to represent the appearance or nature of something. Often called a word picture, description attempts to present its subject for the mind's eye. In doing so, it does not merely become an indifferent camera; instead, it selects details that will depict something well. Just what details the descriptive writer selects will depend on several factors, especially the type of description and the dominant impression in the passage.

Types of Description

On the basis of treatment of subject material, description is customarily divided into two types: objective and subjective.

Effective objective description presents the subject clearly and directly as it exists outside the realm of feelings. If you are explaining the function of the heart, the characteristics of a computer chip, or the renovation of a manufacturing facility, your description would probably feature specific, impersonal details. Most technical and scientific writing is objective in that sense. It is likely to be practical and utilitarian, making little use of speculation and poetic technique while focusing on details of sight.

Effective subjective description is also concerned with clarity and it may be direct, but it conveys a feeling about the subject and sets a mood while making a point. Because most expression involves personal views, even when it explains by analysis, subjective description (often called "emotional description") has a broader range of uses than objective description.

Descriptive passages can have a combination of objective and subjective description; only the larger context of the passage will reveal the main intent.

Imagery

In order to convey your main concern effectively to readers, you will have to give some sensory impressions. These sensory impressions, collectively called *imagery,* refer to that which can be experienced by the senses—what we can see, smell, taste, hear, and touch.

Subjective description is more likely to use more images and words rich in associations than does objective description. But just as a fine line cannot always be drawn between the objective and the subjective, a fine line cannot always be drawn between word choice in one and in the other. However, we can say with certainty that whatever the type of description, careful word choice will always be important. Consider these points about precise diction:

General and Specific Words/Abstract and Concrete Words

To move from the general to the specific is to move from the whole class or body to the individual(s); for example:

General	Specific	More Specific
food	hamburger	Hefty Burger
mess	grease	oil slicks on table
drink	soda	mug of root beer
odor	smell from grill	smell of frying onions

Words are classified as abstract or concrete depending on what they refer to. *Abstract words* refer to qualities or ideas: *good, ordinary, ultimate, truth, beauty, maturity, love. Concrete words* refer to a substance or things; they have reality: *onions, grease, buns, tables, food.* The specific concrete words, sometimes called *concrete particulars*, often support generalizations effectively and convince the reader of the accuracy of the account.

Dominant Impression

Never try to give all of the details in description; instead, be selective, picking only those that you need to make a dominant impression, always taking into account the knowledge and attitudes of your readers. Remember, description is not photographic. If you wish to describe a person, select only the traits that will project your intended dominant impression. If you wish to describe a landscape, do not give all the details that you might find in a picture; just pick the details that support what you want to say. That extremely important dominant impression is directly linked to your purpose and is created by the choosing and arranging of images, figurative language, and revealing details.

Useful Procedure for Writing Description

Description is seldom static. The framework usually includes some narrative pattern, as shown below.

> What is the subject? (school campus during summer vacation)
>
> What is the dominant impression? (deserted, reminding you of different times)
>
> What is the situation? (Note the natural entry of the narrative: You are walking across campus in early August.)
>
> What is the movement (order) as you present details? (movement through time and space)

ORDER FOR THE DESCRIPTIVE NARRATIVE: TIME AND SPACE

All of the details of the description and narrative must have some order, some sequence. Although the two patterns blend, time is the primary factor for telling a story, and space is the primary factor for describing an object or a scene. The following words will help you order time and space.

- Words indicating time: *first, second, then, soon, finally, while, after, next, later, now, before*
- Words indicating space: *next to, below, under, above, behind, in front of, beyond, in the foreground, in the background, to the left, to the right*

EXAMINING ESSAYS OF DESCRIPTIVE NARRATION
Student Writer

My Banana Car

Maria Varela

To an American youngster, a first car is something to be antici-pated, celebrated, and remembered. It should be the apple of one's eye, but it may be a different fruit. It could be a lemon. Even worse, as was the case for student Maria Varela, it was a "banana car." Recreated here for you, the experience is probably funnier to read about than it was to live through.

Situation   I remember how excited I was right after my sixteenth birthday. <u>My dad was going to buy me a car!</u> I imagined it would be a nice little red car with chrome rims (not hubcaps). It would have a tan interior, a sunroof, and a great stereo system that could be heard blocks away. All my friends would envy me. The good-looking boys would notice me with favor. I would be so popular. After all, the cooler the car, the cooler the car owner.

Conflict   <u>I could not believe what was parked in my driveway when I came home from school that Monday afternoon.</u> It was a 1974 Chevy Monte **Description (sight)** Carlo, the kind that has the great big front end. The car was <u>huge</u>. It could seat forty people if it were a dinner table. To top it off, it was <u>yellow like a banana</u>. As a matter of fact it looked like a banana. I held my breath as I walked slowly toward the car, hoping that it belonged to someone who was visiting. At that moment my father ran out of the house with a big smile on his face. "Well, what do you think?" he said. "Nice, huh?"

I looked at my dad, managed to break a smile, and said weakly, "Yeah, Dad. Thanks."

Struggle (continues through next five paragraphs)

I spent the rest of the afternoon trying to find a good quality on the car. First I looked at the outside. It had ugly hubcaps, the kind you find at Pick-a-Part for ten dollars a set. Worst of all, it had a sticker of a horse's head stuck right on the paint near the trunk. I knew that if I tried to remove it, the paint would come off and leave the outline of a horse's head in another color.

Description (sight)

I opened the driver's door slowly as if something like a weasel might pop out at me from inside. The interior was light brown with dark brown stripes. It smelled like Old Spice. I got an image of the previous owner. He must have been a tall, heavy man who wore cheap cologne and liked horses. I plopped down in the driver's seat and grabbed the steering wheel with both hands. "Great!" My feet barely reached the pedals, and my nose

Description (sight, smell)

was at the same level as the top of the steering wheel. I was a short girl, but at that moment I felt even shorter. I got a fat cushion from the house. I would have to sit on this cushion every time I drove this car. I just hoped that no one noticed I was sitting on a cushion. I could already hear them tease. "Maria's so short, she can't even reach the pedals on her car." "Can you see over the dashboard, Maria?"

As I drove my banana car to school the next day, I saw people staring at me. I knew what they were whispering, "How could she drive that ugly car?" and "I would rather walk," and, this one with much laughter, "I can't wait till she peels out of here."

To make matters worse, the car was expensive to drive and prone to breakage. It would take over thirteen dollars in gas to fill up, and that would last me only four days. One day as I was driving down the street, the muffler came off and started

Description (sound, sight)

dragging on the ground. It made a <u>horrible noise</u>, and <u>sparks were flying everywhere</u>. I knew what they were saying: "The sparkling banana car!" I was a legend. Another time I tried to open the window, but it just plopped down, never to be seen again. I could not

keep anything valuable in the car for fear
that it would be stolen. But, of course, I
did not fear that the car would be stolen.
After all, who would want it!

Because my banana car was so large, it
was very hard to maneuver. Twice I knocked
over our mailbox, which was located at the
side of the driveway. I would break into a
sweat whenever I was forced to parallel park.
The most embarrassing situation occurred the
night my friend Monica and I went out to
Tommy's. Tommy's is a popular restaurant
where all the popular people from our school
hang out. Monica and I decided to chance the
drive-through, but as I tried to maneuver the
large car up the narrow passageway, it got
stuck right in the middle. There was no room
to move backward or forward. I could feel my
ears getting hot from embarrassment. Like the
window, Monica sank down out of sight. The

**Description
(sound)**

people behind me started <u>honking</u>. I could see
the people inside the restaurant looking out
to see what the commotion was all about. I
was ready to cry, but at that moment Danny
Gurrerro, one of the cutest boys from our
school, came over and asked if I needed help.
"Yes, please," I blurted out. He jumped into
the car and managed to maneuver it out of

that tight spot. Before he left, he advised me not to take the drive-through anymore. I accepted his advice.

Every morning as I walked out of my house, I hoped the car would be gone, but my banana car was always there waiting for me to drive it to school. I got a part-time job at Togo's Eatery. I wanted to save money for a new car, but after two years, I still did not

Outcome   have enough for the down payment. <u>One day at dinner, my father announced that since I was so responsible with my Monte Carlo, he would help me buy a new car</u>. I jumped out of my seat and wrapped my arms around him. Then, remembering my last expectation, I backed off. "May I pick the car?" "Yes," he said.

Meaning   <u>Goodbye, banana car.</u>

PROFESSIONAL WRITER

The Pie

Gary Soto

Author and teacher Gary Soto here discusses the time when he gave in to temptation, swapping immediate gratification for ensuing guilt. After committing his act, he returned to his home where he "knew" that others knew. It is the classic story of crime and self-punishment, filtered through childhood perceptions, which, of course, magnify and distort. This is taken from his collection of essays A Summer Life *(1990).*

1   I knew enough about hell to stop me from stealing. I was holy in almost every bone. Some days I recognized the shadows of angels flopping on the backyard grass, and other days I heard faraway messages in the plumbing that howled under-

neath the house when I crawled there looking for something to do.

2   But boredom made me sin. Once, at the German Market, I stood before a rack of pies, my sweet tooth gleaming and the juice of guilt wetting my underarms. I gazed at the nine kinds of pie, pecan and apple being my favorites, although cherry looked good, and my dear, fat-faced chocolate was always a good bet. I nearly wept trying to decide which to steal and, forgetting the flowery dust priests give off, the shadow of angels and the proximity of God howling in the plumbing underneath the house, sneaked a pie behind my coffee-lid frisbee and walked to the door, grinning to the bald grocer whose forehead shone with a window of light.

3   "No one saw," I muttered to myself, the pie like a discus in my hand, and hurried across the street, where I sat on someone's lawn. The sun wavered between the branches of a yellowish sycamore. A squirrel nailed itself high on the trunk, where it forked into two large bark-scabbed limbs. Just as I was going to work my cleanest finger into the pie, a neighbor came out to the porch for his mail. He looked at me, and I got up and headed for home. I raced on skinny legs to my block, but slowed to a quick walk when I couldn't wait any longer. I held the pie to my nose and breathed in its sweetness. I licked some of the crust and closed my eyes as I took a small bite.

4   In my front yard, I leaned against a car fender and panicked about stealing the apple pie. I knew an apple got Eve in deep trouble with snakes because Sister Marie had shown us a film about Adam and Eve being cast into the desert, and what scared me more than falling from grace was being thirsty for the rest of my life. But even that didn't stop me from clawing a chunk from the pie tin and pushing it into the cavern of my mouth. The slop was sweet and gold-colored in the afternoon sun. I laid more pieces on my tongue, wet finger-dripping pieces, until I was finished and felt like crying because it was about the best thing I had ever tasted. I realized right there and then, in my sixth year, in my tiny body of two hundred bones and three or four sins, that the best things in life came stolen. I wiped my sticky fingers on the grass and rolled my tongue over the corners of my mouth. A burp perfumed the air.

5   I felt bad not sharing with Cross-Eyed Johnny, a neighbor kid. He stood over my shoulder and asked, "Can I have some?" Crust fell from my mouth, and my teeth were bathed with the

jam-like filling. Tears blurred my eyes as I remembered the grocer's forehead. I remembered the other pies on the rack, the warm air of the fan above the door and the car that honked as I crossed the street without looking.

6   "Get away," I had answered Cross-Eyed Johnny. He watched my fingers greedily push big chunks of pie down my throat. He swallowed and said in a whisper, "Your hands are dirty," then returned home to climb his roof and sit watching me eat the pie by myself. After a while, he jumped off and hobbled away because the fall had hurt him.

7   I sat on the curb. The pie tin glared at me and rolled away when the wind picked up. My face was sticky with guilt. A car honked, and the driver knew. Mrs. Hancock stood on her lawn, hands on hip, and she knew. My mom, peeling a mountain of potatoes at the Redi-Spud factory, knew. I got to my feet, stomach taut, mouth tired of chewing, and flung my frisbee across the street, its shadow like the shadow of an angel fleeing bad deeds. I retrieved it, jogging slowly. I flung it again until I was bored and thirsty.

8   I returned home to drink water and help my sister glue bottle caps onto cardboard, a project for summer school. But the bottle caps bored me, and the water soon filled me up more than the pie. With the kitchen stifling with heat and lunatic flies, I decided to crawl underneath our house and lie in the cool shadows listening to the howling sounds of plumbing. Was it God? Was it Father, speaking from death, or Uncle with his last shiny dime? I listened, ear pressed to a cold pipe, and heard a howl like the sea. I lay until I was cold and then crawled back to the light, rising from one knee, then another, to dust off my pants and squint in the harsh light. I looked and saw the glare of a pie tin on a hot day. I knew sin was what you take and didn't give back.

EXERCISE 1

1. Using key words and phrases from Soto's story, explain the narrative pattern of this account. Comment on each of the five narrative properties:

    Situation

    Conflict

Struggle

Outcome

Meaning

2. The narrator steals the pie, breaking the social order by violating the storeowner's rights. He also goes against what he knows is right, violating his own conscience. How are these two points of conflict related? What would happen to the story if the second violation hadn't occurred?

3. What form does the narrator's guilt take? How is description used to show that guilt?

4. How realistic is this story of youthful crime and self-punishment?

PRACTICING PATTERNS OF DESCRIPTIVE NARRATION

EXERCISE 2

Fill in the blanks to complete the pattern of descriptive narration.

Topic: last-minute shopping for a present

    I. _____ (a certain department in a mall store)

      A. Other shoppers

        1. _____ (appearance)

        2. _____ (behavior)

  B. Condition and arrangement of merchandise (describe with appropriate details of imagery: sight, sound, taste, smell, touch)

  1. _____

  2. _____

  3. _____

II. Can't find a particular item

  A. Search and search

  B. Start getting frustrated

  C. Meet an old friend (perhaps the person you are shopping for)

  1. _____ (description of friend)

  2. _____ (more description, perhaps adding person in action)

III. _____ (whatever the friend does to help)

  A. _____

  B. _____

IV. _____ (what you purchase or what you decide to do)

  A. _____

  B. _____

TOPICS FOR ESSAYS OF DESCRIPTIVE NARRATION

Reading-Related Topics

1. "My Banana Car": Write about your first (or any other) car, one that you came to prize or despise. Include detailed description along with a narrative about your car and your life at that particular time.
2. Interview someone and write about that person's first car.
3. Write a descriptive narrative about any object you have especially liked or disliked.

4. "The Pie": Write an essay of descriptive narration about a childhood experience in which you did something wrong or perceived that you did.
5. Write about Soto's escapade from the pie's point of view.

Career-Related Topics

6. Write a descriptive narrative about an event at work that was exceedingly satisfying or unsatisfying.
7. Describe a person performing a job in a stressful situation. Point out what the person did that was right and wrong.
8. Write about your best or worst moment searching for a job, being interviewed for a job, or training for a job. Focus on a brief period of time so that you can include descriptive detail.

General Topics

Write a descriptive narrative about one of the following subjects. Limit the time frame so that you can include descriptive detail.

9. A ceremony such as a graduation, funeral, or wedding
10. A time when you made a proposal for marriage (or received one) or applied for a position you wanted
11. A time when you confronted authority or had to deliver bad news
12. Your first date, first day in a new school, first public performance, first time in love
13. The time you met (saw) a most impressive doctor, teacher, speaker, singer, irritating person, salesperson, or police officer
14. The occasion when you witnessed an accident or a natural disaster such as a tornado or flood

WRITER'S GUIDELINES AT A GLANCE: DESCRIPTIVE NARRATION

Narration

1. Include these points to be sure you have a complete narrative.

   Situation
   Conflict
   Struggle
   Outcome
   Meaning

2. Consider using dialogue.
3. Give details concerning action.

Description

1. In an objective description, use direct, practical language and appeal mainly to the sense of sight.
2. In an emotional description, appeal to the reader's feelings, especially through images of sight, sound, smell, taste, and touch.
3. Use specific and concrete words if appropriate.
4. Relate your details to the dominant impression of your description.

Descriptive Narrative

1. All of your details must have an order or sequence. Although the two patterns blend, time is the primary factor for telling a story, whereas space is the primary factor for description.

   - Words indicating time: *first, second, then, soon, finally, while, after, next, later, now, before*
   - Words indicating space: *next to, below, under, above, behind, in front of, beyond, in the foreground, in the background, to the left, to the right*

2. Both description and narration in college writing usually have an expository purpose; that is, they explain a specified or implied idea.

5

Exemplification: Writing with Examples

WRITING ESSAYS OF EXEMPLIFICATION

Exemplification means using examples to explain, convince, or amuse. Lending interest and information to writing, exemplification is one of the most common and effective ways of developing ideas. Examples may be developed in as much as a paragraph or more, or they may be phrases or only single words, as in the following sentence: "Children like packaged breakfast foods, such as *Wheaties, Cheerios*, and *Rice Krispies.*"

Characteristics of Good Examples

As supporting information, the best examples are vivid, specific, and representative. These three qualities are closely linked; collectively, they must support the topic sentence of a paragraph and the thesis of the essay. The *vivid* example attracts attention. Through a memorable presentation and the use of identifying names, the example becomes *specific* to the reader. A good example must also be *representative*; that is, it must be experienced as typical, so that it can be the basis for a generalization.

Finally, and most important, the connection between the example and the thesis must be clear. A bizarre case of cheating may be fascinating in itself (vivid and specific), but in an essay on "the hard work of cheating," it must also support (represent) the thesis. The reader should say, in effect, "That's interesting, convincing, and memorable. Though it's unusual, I can see that it's typical of what goes on."

Techniques for Finding Examples

Writing a good essay of exemplification begins, as always, with prewriting. The techniques you use will depend on what you are

67

writing about. Assuming that you begin with a topic idea, one useful technique is listing. Base your list on what you have read, heard, and experienced. Here is a list on the topic "the hard work of cheating":

The two times when I cheated

- Copied homework
- Brought in list for a biology test
- Guilt

A person who bought a research paper
Jess, who copied from me
The Internet "Cheaters" source
The two persons who exchanged identities
More work than it's worth
More stress than it's worth

Connecting Examples with Purpose

In the following student essay, "Cheating Is Not Worth the Bother," Lara Olivas uses examples effectively by stating the purpose of the essay (thesis), connecting the thesis to the topic sentences, and then supporting each topic sentence with one or more examples distinguished with specific, interesting details.

EXAMINING ESSAYS OF EXEMPLIFICATION

Student Writer

Cheating Is Not Worth the Bother

Lara Olivas

Lara Olivas calls herself an expert in cheating—not because she is a cheater, but because she has seen cheating take place for most of her life. What is the best reason for not cheating: that the cheater might get caught—or that the cheater doesn't learn? The main reason she gives is neither. Read on.

I knew many students who took college
prep classes all the way through high school
and never read a book in an English class.
They read Cliff's Notes or Monarch Notes, or

they copied work from other people who did.
But they weren't cheating just in English
classes. They had systems of cheating in
every class. Cheating became a way of life.
They were always conniving and scheming. I'm
not that pure. I've tried cheating, but I
soon rejected it. I didn't learn that way,
and I lost my self-esteem. I also feared
getting caught; and I discovered that most of
the time cheating was hard, stressful work.
So I never became, like some of my friends, a
master cheater, but I did become a master
observer of cheaters because students almost

Thesis   always see more than teachers do. <u>What I</u>
<u>learned was that cheaters often put</u>
<u>themselves under more stress than honest</u>
<u>students</u>.

Topic
sentence   <u>Even the student who pays for school work</u>
<u>can become a victim of stress</u>. <u>I remember a</u>
<u>student in my junior composition class who</u>

Specific
example   <u>needed a research paper</u>, so he found a source
and bought one for seventy-five dollars. The
<u>first trouble</u> was that he had to submit the
work in stages: the topic, the working
bibliography, the note cards, the outline,

Order by time   the rough draft, and the final. <u>Therefore</u>, he
went to the library and started working
backwards. Of course, he couldn't turn in

only the bib cards actually used in the
paper, and <u>next</u> he had to make out note cards
for the material he "would be" documenting,
and even make out more. <u>After</u> having all
kinds of trouble, he realized that the bought
paper was of "A" quality, whereas he had been
a "C" student. He went back to his source and
was told he should change the sentence
structure and so on to make the paper weaker.
<u>Finally</u> he dropped the class after spending
more time on his paper than I did on mine.
He also suffered more anxiety than the
students who put in the most work on their
papers.

**Topic
sentence**
<u>Then during my senior year, a female
student in Biology 4 became another subject
for my study in cheating</u>. She was sitting
next to me, so I could see everything she

**Specific
example**
did. <u>She kept her cheat cards in her bra</u>.
This is the way she did it. <u>On the day of the
test</u>, she would wear a loose-fitting blouse

Order by time
or dress. <u>Then</u> when the instructor wasn't
watching, she would hunch her shoulders like
a buzzard sleeping and slump so she could
look down the front of her own dress.
<u>Sometimes</u> she'd have to fiddle around down
there to get the cheat card to pop into

place. Her writing was tiny. I know about the writing because one day the teacher left the room, and she just took a card out and used it openly. If the instructor stared at her when she was looking down, she would blow inside her dress as if she were trying to cool off her bosom or something. Then she would smile at the instructor and shake her head and pucker her lips to show how hot it was. Her strategy worked because she did perspire due to the stress. The tests were mainly on muscles and bones and weren't that difficult. She probably worked harder in rigging the cheat cards on her underwear than I did in memorizing information.

There were dozens of other examples—the

Cluster of examples writing on seats, hands, arms, legs, and cuffs; the hand signs, blinks, and coughs; and the plagiarism of all kinds. There were even the classes where cheating would never be caught because some teachers didn't watch carefully during the tests, and others didn't read carefully later. But for the most part,

Restated thesis the cheaters were the ones who had the most anxiety and often the ones who did the most work—work that was never directed toward learning.

PROFESSIONAL WRITER

Spanglish

Janice Castro, with Dan Cook and Cristina Garcia

When people of two cultures and two languages come together, the most natural of blends is that of language. In the United States, that idea has been explored extensively by linguists, who have documented just how the migration of people from different regions to states such as California has resulted in the blending of dialects. For example, in California a person may give a Southern pronunciation to the word apricot. ("A pri cot" rather than "ap ri cot") and a Northern pronunciation to the word blouse ("blous" rather than "blouz"). Phrases also get mixed. As shown in the following essay, the same occurs with Spanish and English.

1   In Manhattan a first-grader greets her visiting grandparents, happily exclaiming, "Come here, *siéntate!*" Her bemused grandfather, who does not speak Spanish, nevertheless knows she is asking him to sit down. A Miami personnel officer understands what a job applicant means when he says, "*Quiero un part time.*" Nor do drivers miss a beat reading a billboard alongside a Los Angeles street advertising CERVEZA—SIX-PACK!

2   This free-form blend of Spanish and English, known as Spanglish, is common linguistic currency wherever concentrations of Hispanic Americans are found in the U.S. In Los Angeles, where 55% of the city's 3 million inhabitants speak Spanish, Spanglish is as much a part of daily life as sunglasses. Unlike the broken-English efforts of earlier immigrants from Europe, Asia and other regions, Spanglish has become a widely accepted conversational mode used casually—even playfully—by Spanish-speaking immigrants and native-born Americans alike.

3   Consisting of one part Hispanicized English, one part Americanized Spanish and more than a little fractured syntax, Spanglish is a bit like a Robin Williams comedy routine: a crackling line of cross-cultural patter straight from the melting pot. Often it enters Anglo homes and families through the children, who pick it up at school or at play with their young Hispanic contemporaries. In other cases, it comes from watching TV; many an Anglo child watching *Sesame Street* has learned *uno dos tres* almost as quickly as one two three.

4   Spanglish takes a variety of forms, from the Southern California Anglos who bid farewell with the utterly silly "*hasta la*

bye-bye" to the Cuban-American drivers in Miami who *par-quean* their *carros*. Some Spanglish sentences are mostly Spanish, with a quick detour for an English word or two. A Latino friend may cut short a conversation by glancing at his watch and excusing himself with the explanation that he must *"ir al supermarket."*

5   Many of the English words transplanted in this way are simply handier than their Spanish counterparts. No matter how distasteful the subject, for example, it is still easier to say "income tax" than *impuesto sobre la renta*. At the same time, many Spanish-speaking immigrants have adopted such terms as VCR, microwave and dishwasher for what they view as largely American phenomena. Still other English words convey a cultural context that is not implicit in the Spanish. A friend who invites you to *lonche* most likely has in mind the brisk American custom of "doing lunch" rather than the languorous afternoon break traditionally implied by *almuerzo*.

6   Mainstream Americans exposed to similar hybrids of German, Chinese or Hindi might by mystified. But even Anglos who speak little or no Spanish are somewhat familiar with Spanglish. Living among them, for one thing, are 19 million Hispanics. In addition, more American high school and university students sign up for Spanish than for any other foreign language.

7   Only in the past ten years, though, has Spanglish begun to turn into a national slang. Its popularity has grown with the explosive increases in U.S. immigration from Latin American countries. English has increasingly collided with Spanish in retail stores, offices and classrooms, in pop music and on street corners. Anglos whose ancestors picked up such Spanish words as *rancho, bronco, tornado* and *incommunicado*, for instance, now freely use such Spanish words as *gracias, bueno, amigo* and *por favor*.

8   Among Latinos, Spanglish conversations often flow easily from Spanish into several sentences of English and back.

9   Spanglish is a sort of code for Latinos: the speakers know Spanish, but their hybrid language reflects the American culture in which they live. Many lean to shorter, clipped phrases in place of the longer, more graceful expressions their parents used. Says Leonel de la Cuesta, an assistant professor of modern languages at Florida International University in Miami: "In the U.S., time is money, and that is showing up in Spanglish as an

economy of language." Conversational examples: *taipiar* (type) and *winshi-wiper* (windshield wiper) replace *escribir a maquina* and *limpiaparabrisas*.

10   Major advertisers, eager to tap the estimated $134 billion in spending power wielded by Spanish-speaking Americans, have ventured into Spanglish to promote their products. In some cases, attempts to sprinkle Spanish through commercials have produced embarrassing gaffes. A Braniff airlines ad that sought to tell Spanish-speaking audiences they could settle back *en* (in) luxuriant *cuero* (leather) seats, for example, inadvertently said they could fly without clothes (*encuero*). A fractured translation of the Miller Lite slogan told readers the beer was "Filling, and less delicious." Similar blunders are often made by Anglos trying to impress Spanish-speaking pals. But if Latinos are amused by mangled Spanglish, they also recognize these goofs as a sort of friendly acceptance. As they might put it, *no problema*.

EXERCISE 1

1. Why do people change and blend languages?

2. How do such changes occur?

3. Why are mistakes tolerated so easily, according to the authors of "Spanglish"?

4. Write the numbers of the three paragraphs that have no examples.

    _____ _____ _____

5. Explain why clusters of examples are more appropriate than extended examples for this essay.

PRACTICING PATTERNS OF EXEMPLIFICATION

EXERCISE 2

Fill in the blanks to add (more) examples that support the thesis.

1. Thesis: Some people let television watching interfere with their social lives.

    I. Watching football games at a family gathering on holidays

    II. Watching television in a _____

    III. _____

2. Thesis: Most successful movies are more concerned with action than character, and the action is violent.

    I. (Name of movie) _____

    II. (Name of movie) _____

    III. (Name of movie) _____

TOPICS FOR ESSAYS OF EXEMPLIFICATION

Reading-Related Topics

1. "Cheating Is Not Worth the Bother": Retain the main idea (or alter it to whatever extent you choose) of Olivas' essay as your thesis and use your own examples to develop an essay.
2. Write an essay about electronic sources, such as the Internet and small computers, that are used in cheating.

3. Write about how friends, clubs, businesses, and fraternal organizations sometimes exchange, sell, collect, and distribute information for cheating.

4. "Spanglish": If you are from a region in which Spanglish is spoken, do your own comparative study of Spanglish and your native language, complete with comments on causes, occasions for usage, and reaction to the blends.

5. Write about a blend of class or group dialects that occur because of the influence of music and movies (rap, reggae, and so on). Give specific examples.

6. In an essay apply the idea of blending to another aspect of culture, such as dress, home furnishings, diets, or behavior.

7. If you are from a family with racial, class, or regional differences, discuss how different aspects of culture, such as dress, home furnishings, diets, speech, or behavior, sometimes clash and sometimes blend.

Career-Related Topics

Use specific examples to support one of the following statements as applied to business, work, or career preparation.

8. My chosen career field requires much preparation.

9. If I had been the boss at the place where I work, I would have handled certain situations differently.

10. "Burning bridges" should be done in warfare, not in work situations.

11. In some places where I worked (or went to school), sexual harassment occurred on an almost daily basis.

12. Sometimes one does a lot of "tongue-biting" and "pride-swallowing" when dealing with irate customers.

13. The women managers I know have really had to prove their competency.

General Topics

Develop an essay mainly by using examples to support one of these thesis statements.

14. We are surrounded by people with bad manners.

15. Most of what I really like is bad for me or someone else.

16. I am trying to live with certain problems I can't solve.

17. Some of our modern conveniences are causing some of our biggest problems.

18. One can tell much about people by the way they eat (or dress, talk, react to stressful situations, relate to their family and friends).
19. I would be happier if I could divorce some of my relatives.
20. Some people who think they are nonconformists are conforming to their own group.
21. College (or staying at home, working full-time, having a large family, getting married) is not for everyone.

WRITER'S GUIDELINES AT A GLANCE: EXEMPLIFICATION

1. Use examples to explain, convince, or amuse.
2. Use examples that are vivid, specific, and representative.

   - Vivid examples attract attention.
   - Specific examples are identifiable.
   - Representative examples are typical and therefore the basis for generalization.

3. Tie your examples clearly to your thesis.
4. Draw your examples from what you have read, heard, and experienced.
5. Brainstorm a list of possible examples before you write.

6

Analysis by Division: Examining the Parts

WRITING ESSAYS OF ANALYSIS BY DIVISION

If you need to explain how something works or exists as a unit, you will write an analysis by division. You will break down a unit (your subject) into its parts and explain how each part functions in relation to the operation or existence of the whole. The most important word here is *unit*. You begin with something that can stand alone or can be regarded separately: a poem, a heart, a painting, a car, a bike, a person, a school, a committee. The following procedure will guide you in writing an analysis by division. Move from subject to principle, to division, to relationship.

> Step 1: Begin with something that is a unit.
> Step 2: State one principle by which the unit can function.
> Step 3: Divide the unit into parts according to that principle.
> Step 4: Discuss each of the parts in relation to the unit.

Here's how this general procedure is applied to a real object (unit).

> Step 1: For the unit, we choose a pencil.
> Step 2: For our principle (the perceived purpose or role), we see the pencil as a writing instrument.
> Step 3: For dividing the unit into parts based on the principle of a pencil as a writing instrument, we divide the pencil into an eraser, an eraser holder, a wooden barrel, and a thin graphite core with a sharpened point.
> Step 4: For our discussion of the parts in relation to the unit, we can say something like this: "At the top of the wooden barrel is a strip of metal encircling an eraser and clamping it to the barrel. In the center of the barrel is a core of graphite that can be sharpened to a point at the end and

used for writing. The eraser is used to remove marks made by the graphite point. Thus we have a complete writing tool, one that marks and erases marks."

Like many things, a pencil can be regarded in different ways. For example, an artist might not consider a pencil mainly as a writing tool. Instead, an artist might look at a pencil and see it as an object of simple functional beauty that could be used as a subject in a still-life painting. Here is how an artist might follow the procedure.

> Step 1: For the unit, I choose a pencil.
> Step 2: For the principle or way of regarding the unit, I see the pencil as an object of simple functional beauty.
> Step 3: For the division into parts based on my principle, I divide the pencil into texture, shape, and color.
> Step 4: For the discussion of parts in relation to the unit, I will explain how the textures of the metal, graphite, and wood, along with their shapes and colors, produce a beautiful object.

Either treatment of the same unit, the pencil, is valid. But mixing the treatments by applying more than one principle at a time causes problems. For example, if we were to say that a pencil has an eraser, an eraser holder, a wooden barrel, a graphite core, and a beautiful coat of yellow paint, we would have an illogical analysis by division, because all parts but the "beautiful coat of yellow paint" relate to the pencil as a writing instrument.

Organization

In an essay of analysis by division, the main parts are likely to be the main points of your outline or main extensions of your cluster. If they are anything else, reconsider your organization. For the pencil, your outline might look like this:

I. Eraser
II. Eraser holder
III. Wooden barrel
IV. Graphite core with point at one end

Sequence of Parts

The order in which you discuss the parts will vary according to the nature of the unit and the way in which you view it. Here are some possible sequences for organizing the parts of a unit.

Time: The sequence of the parts in your essay can be mainly chronological, or time-based (if you are dealing with something that functions on its own, such as a heart, with the parts presented in relation to stages of the function).

Space: If your unit is a visual object, especially if, like the pencil, it does nothing by itself, you may discuss the parts in relation to space. In the example above, the parts of the pencil begin at the top with the eraser and end at the bottom with the pencil point.

Emphasis: Since the most emphatic part of any piece of writing is the end (the second most emphatic point is the beginning), consider placing the most significant part of the unit at the end. In the example, both space and emphasis govern the placement of the pencil point at the end of the order.

EXAMINING ESSAYS OF ANALYSIS BY DIVISION

Student Writer

More Than Book 'Em

Jerry Price

A veteran police officer of fifteen years, Jerry Price knows well that every call has its unique characteristics, so he must be much more than a simple cop. Here he discusses the different roles he might assume when he answers a call concerning a family dispute.

As a police officer, when I am on patrol I have a wide variety of duties. I respond to

Unit   several different types of calls. One of the most common calls involves a family dispute

Principle   between a husband and wife. When I respond to that kind of problem, I have to play one or more quite different roles. The common roles for family disputes are counselor, referee,

Thesis (parts)   and law enforcer.

The most common family dispute involves a

Topic sentence (part 1) husband and wife arguing. <u>Usually the argument is almost over when I arrive, and I need to talk to both sides</u>. Depending on how intense they are, I either separate them or talk to them together. Both the husband and wife will tell me they are right and the other spouse is wrong. I then become a <u>counselor</u>. In this role I must be a good listener to both parties, and when they are done talking, it's my turn to talk. In the worst situation I may tell them it looks as if they are headed for a separation or divorce. However, most of the time I tell them to act like adults and talk to their spouse as they talked to me. I may suggest that they seek professional counseling. With the husband and wife now having everything off their chests, and after their having received my small lecture, they may be able to go back to living relatively peaceful lives together.

Topic sentence (part 2) <u>In a different scenario, if the yelling and screaming is still going on when I arrive, I may want to just stand back and be a referee</u>. I usually allow the wife to talk first. She typically tells her husband off. Not forgetting my role as referee, I step in only if the argument gets extremely ugly. When this happens, I send the wife to a neutral corner to cool off. Then I allow her to continue her verbal assault. When I feel the husband has had enough, I stop the wife and give the husband a turn. All the time I am watching and listening. My main task is to keep the fight clean. If I think progress is being made with the couple, I let it continue. If the argument is going in circles, I may stop the fight. At this time I may send one of the fighters out for a drive or to a friend's house to cool off. This diversion is, however, only a temporary solution to the problem, for when the couple gets back together I will probably be needed for round two.

Topic sentence (part 3) When the family dispute turns into a fist fight, it's usually the husband hitting his wife. Wives do hit their husbands, but the male ego won't let men call the police. When the husband has hit his wife, and she has only a very minor injury, it will be up to her to have her husband arrested. If the wife is bleeding or has several bruises, then I make the decision. In these cases I become the enforcer of the law. I always place the husband under arrest even if the wife doesn't

want it. As the enforcer I then take the
husband to jail. The severity of the wife's
injuries will determine how long the husband
will stay in jail. He may be released in a
couple of hours with a ticket and a court
date, or he can be in jail until he can be
seen by a judge. Prior convictions and
restraining orders are considerations.

As a typical police officer on patrol, I
make many decisions and play many roles in
domestic disturbance cases. The circumstances
of these cases dictate the way each is
handled. <u>As an experienced officer, I should
be able to make the right decision, and I
should know when to be a counselor, a</u>

**Restated
thesis** <u>referee, or a law enforcer</u>.

PROFESSIONAL WRITER

Total Institutions

Seymour Feshbach and Bernard Weiner

In their book Personality, *Feshbach and Weiner are concerned especially with physical, social, and cultural determinants of personality and behavior. Here they examine the total institution and divide it into unique parts. The main analysis by division occurs in the second paragraph, the central part of this essay.*

1 A total institution completely encompasses the individual,
forming a barrier to the types of social intercourse that occur
outside such a setting. Monasteries, jails, homes for the aged,
boarding schools, and military academies are a few examples of
total institutions.

2   Total institutions have certain common characteristics. First, the individuals in such environments must sleep, play, and work within the same setting. These are generally segmented spheres of activity in the lives of most individuals, but within a total institution one sphere of activity overlaps with others. Second, each phase of life takes place in the company of a large group of others. Frequently, sleeping is done in a barracks, food is served in a cafeteria, and so on. In such activities everyone is treated alike and must perform certain essential tasks. Third, activities in an institution are tightly scheduled according to a master plan, with set times to rise, to eat, to exercise, and to sleep. These institutional characteristics result in a bureaucratic society, which requires the hiring of other people for surveillance. What often results is a dichotomous split in the groups within an institution into a large, managed group (*inmates*) and a small supervisory staff. There tends to be great social distance between the groups, who perceive each other according to stereotypes and have severely restricted communications.

3   The world of the inmate differs greatly from the outside world. When one enters a total institution, all previous roles, such as father or husband, are disrupted. The individual is further depersonalized by the issuance of a uniform, confiscation of belongings, and gathering of personal information, as well as by more subtle touches like doorless toilets, record keeping, and bedchecks. The effects of an institutional setting are so all-encompassing that one can meaningfully speak of an "institutional personality": a persistent manner of behaving compliantly and without emotional involvement.

4   Of course, there are individual differences in adaptation to the situation. They can be as extreme as psychosis, childlike regression, and depression or as mild as resigned compliance. Most individuals do adjust and build up a system of satisfactions, such as close friendships and cliques. But because of these bonds and the fact that the habits needed to function in the outside world have been lost, inmates face great problems upon leaving an institution. A shift from the top of a small society to the bottom of a larger one may be further demoralizing.

5   To understand behavior, the environment in which it occurs must be taken into consideration.

EXERCISE 1

1. What barrier does the individual in the total institution face?

2. What are the three common characteristics (the parts of the analysis by division) of the total institution (paragraph 2)?

3. What is an institutional personality?

4. What are some of the adaptations to the total institution?

5. Some essays of analysis by division use the parts for the major pattern of the essay; others combine analysis by division with other forms of writing. Explain how the lengthy paragraph 2 relates to paragraphs 3 and 4.

PRACTICING PATTERNS OF ANALYSIS BY DIVISION

▌ EXERCISE 2

Fill in the blanks to complete each analysis by division.

1. Unit: Doctor

2. Principle: Effective as a general practitioner

3. Parts based on the principle:

    I. Ability to _____

    II. Knowledge of _____

    III. Knowledge of <u>computers and other equipment</u>

1. Unit: Newspaper

2. Principle: Sections for readers

3. Parts based on the principle:

    I. News

    II. _____

    III. _____

    IV. _____

    V. _____

TOPICS FOR ESSAYS OF ANALYSIS BY DIVISION

Reading-Related Topics

1. "More Than Book 'Em": Using Price's basic idea that he must be flexible and respond to the needs of the people he deals with, write about how you, in some function, must also fulfill several roles. Consider such roles as parent, family, member, friend, employee, referee, guide, spouse, and student.

2. Write about someone else's multiple roles, such as those mentioned in the previous suggestion.

3. "Total Institutions": Write an essay in which you apply the characteristics of the total institution to some setting you are

familiar with (such as a school, jail, convalescent home, military service, a particular family) through direct or indirect experience.

Career-Related Topics

4. Explain how the parts of a particular product function together as a unit.
5. Explain how each of several qualities of a specific person—such as his or her intelligence, sincerity, knowledgeability, ability to communicate, manner, attitude, and appearance—makes that individual an effective salesperson, manager, or employee.
6. Explain how the demands or requirements for a particular job represent a comprehensive picture of that job.
7. Explain how the aspects of a particular service (such as friendly, competent, punctual, confidential) work together in a satisfactory manner.

General Topics

Some of the following topics are too broad for an essay and should be narrowed. For example, the general "a wedding ceremony" could be narrowed to the particular "José and Maria's wedding ceremony."

8. An organ in the human body
9. A machine such as an automobile, a computer, a camera
10. A ceremony—wedding, graduation
11. A holiday celebration, a pep rally, a sales convention, a religious revival
12. An offensive team in football (any team in any game)
13. A family, a relationship, a gang, a club, a sorority, a fraternity
14. An album, a performance, a song, a singer, an actor, a musical group, a musical instrument
15. A movie, a television program, a video game
16. Any well-known person—athlete, politician, criminal, writer

Writer's Guidelines at a Glance: Analysis by Division

Almost anything can be analyzed by division—for example, how the parts of the ear work in hearing, how the parts of the eye work in seeing, or how the parts of the heart work in pumping blood throughout the body. Subjects such as these are all approached with the same systematic procedure.

1. This is the procedure.

   - *Step 1.* Begin with something that is a unit.
   - *Step 2.* State the principle by which that unit functions.
   - *Step 3.* Divide the unit into parts according to the principle.
   - *Step 4.* Discuss each of the parts in relation to the unit.

2. This is the way you might apply that procedure to a good boss.

▪ Unit	Manager
▪ Principle of function	Effective as a leader
▪ Parts based on the principle	Fair, intelligent, stable, competent in field
▪ Discussion	Consider each part in relation to person's effectiveness as a manager.

3. This is how a basic outline of analysis by division might look.

   Thesis: To be effective as a leader, a manager needs specific qualities.

   I. Fair
   II. Intelligent
   III. Stable
   IV. Competent in field

7

Process Analysis: Writing About Doing

WRITING ESSAYS OF PROCESS ANALYSIS

If you have any doubt about how frequently we use process analysis, just think about how many times you have heard people say, "How do you do it?" or "How is [was] it done?" Even when you are not hearing those questions, you are posing them yourself when you need to make something, cook a meal, assemble an item, take some medicine, repair something, or figure out what happened. In your college classes, you may have to discover how osmosis occurs, how a rock changes form, how a mountain was formed, how a battle was won, or how a bill goes through the legislature.

If you need to explain how to do something or how something was (is) done, you will write a paper of *process analysis.* You will break down your topic into stages, explaining each so that your reader can duplicate or understand the process.

Two Types of Process Analysis: Directive and Informative

The questions How do I do it? and How is (was) it done? will lead you into two different types of process analysis—directive and informative.

Directive process analysis explains how to do something. As the name suggests, it gives directions and tells the reader how to do something. It says, for example, "Read me, and you can bake a pie (tune up your car, read a book, write an essay, take some medicine)." Because it is presented directly to the reader, it usually addresses the reader as "you," or it implies the "you" by saying something such as "First [you] purchase a large, fat wombat, and then [you] . . . " In the same way, this textbook addresses you or implies "you" because it is a long how-to-do-it (directive process analysis) statement.

Informative process analysis explains how something was (is) done by giving data (information). Whereas the directive process analysis tells you what to do in the future, the informative process analysis tells you what has occurred or what is occurring. If it is something in nature, such as the formation of a mountain, you can read and understand the process by which it emerged. In this type of process analysis, you do not tell the reader what to do; therefore, you do not use the words *you* or *your*.

Working with Stages

Preparation   In the first stage of the directive type of process analysis, list the materials or equipment needed for the process and discuss the necessary setup arrangements. For some topics, this stage will also provide technical terms and definitions. The degree to which this stage is detailed will depend on both the subject itself and the expected knowledge and experience of the projected audience.

The informative type of process analysis may begin with background or context rather than with preparation. For example, a statement explaining how mountains form might begin with a description of a flat portion of the earth made up of plates that are arranged like a jigsaw puzzle.

Steps   The actual process will be presented here. Each step must be explained clearly and directly, and phrased to accommodate the audience. The language, especially in directive process analysis, is likely to be simple and concise; however, avoid dropping words such as *and, a, an, the* and *of*, and thereby lapsing into "recipe language." The steps may be accompanied by explanations about why certain procedures are necessary and how not following directions carefully can lead to trouble.

Order   The order will usually be chronological (time based) in some sense. Certain transitional words are commonly used to promote coherence: *first, second, third, then, soon, now, next, finally, at last, therefore, consequently,* and—especially for informative process analysis—words used to show the passage of time such as hours, days of the week, and so on.

Basic Forms

- Consider using this form for the directive process (with topics such as how to cook something or how to fix something).

    I. Preparation
       A.
       B.
       C.
    II. Steps
       A.
       B.
       C.
       D.

- Consider using this form for the informative process (with topics such as how a volcano functions or how a battle was won).

    I. Background or context
       A.
       B.
       C.
    II. Change or development (narrative)
       A.
       B.
       C.
       D.

EXAMINING ESSAYS OF PROCESS ANALYSIS

Student Writer

Guarding a Wide Receiver

Brian Landry

Watching football games, most of us have observed cornerbacks harassing wide receivers. One person wants to catch the ball thrown by the quarterback; however, an opponent is there to interfere. In this essay Brian Landry, a former high school football player, explains that the successful cornerback is doing much more than being annoying; he is actually playing a game within a game.

Unlike golf, one of the ultimate

individual sports, football is a team sport,

and many people think of it as one machine facing off against another. What those people miss is that each player has a specific role, and often an individual player is engaged in a game within a game against another player who is executing his own battle plan. Few match-ups offer more challenges to individuals than the one between the cornerback and the wide receiver. <u>As a</u>

Thesis   <u>cornerback, I finally discovered an effective process, one that begins with preparation before the game and ends with strategic action on the field during a pass play.</u>

Preparation   <u>The most important part of winning is in the preparation. First, you need to be mentally and physically fit.</u> Mental fitness involves studying your opposing team and their strategies, as well as knowing your own defensive schemes and having a winning attitude. Physical fitness is self-explanatory. You must have stamina, strength, and speed. <u>Next is equipment</u>. You must wear the appropriate gear and, especially, the shoes that suit the playing surface. With that preparation completed, you are ready for the wide receiver poised just across the line from you, his mind focused on making you look foolish on the next pass play.

Step 1 <u>Initially you must control the distance between yourself and the receiver</u>. Before the ball is snapped, keep yourself five to ten yards from the receiver, depending on his speed. If the receiver is fast, you can either give him a couple of yards distance so it will neutralize his speed, or you can bump him at the line so he doesn't get to use his speed. When the ball is about to be hiked, if you know the receiver is slow, get close to him, about one yard away. Always keep your feet shoulder-wide apart. Crouch down slightly, bringing your weight over your toes. This should be a very balanced position. Look the receiver in the eyes and try to intimidate him.

Step 2 <u>Body contact should be just right, not too much or too little</u>. When the ball is snapped, thrust your arms forward, striking the receiver just below his shoulder pads, making sure you are maintaining balance. If this is accomplished, then try to keep him there. Avoid grasping, because this will cause a penalty. More often than not, the receiver will move to avoid this procedure. Do not let him get inside of you. Push him towards the sidelines. Now you need to turn with him, keeping him within touching distance. You want to be between him and the quarterback. Try to remain always in contact with him. Use your outside arm for this procedure. Don't push him too much after five yards because this is another penalty.

Step 3   Your eyes now become your main tools. Look into the receiver's eyes, watching his reactions. Don't get in front of him because he can then stop and turn back. Watch his moves and be his shadow. Remember to keep your balance so you can turn quickly when he does. As you are watching his eyes, you are looking for two things. If his eyes become extremely big, as if a present is coming his way, or they become fixed on an object, then you must react quickly. This means the ball is usually en route there. Turn your head away from the receiver and back toward the quarterback. Pick up the ball as quickly as possible, still keeping in touch with the receiver, with your outside arm.

Step 4   At some point you may play the ball as well as the receiver. Once you see the ball, if it is off target with the receiver, run to where it is headed and catch it. If it is coming in your direction, don't let the receiver get between you and the ball. Judge the distance, and when the ball is close

enough for you to jump and catch it, do so.
Always catch the ball at its highest point.
This technique keeps a receiver from stealing
it at the last second. Remember that the
receiver is trying for the ball too. You must
want it more than he does. If the receiver has
positioned himself in front of you, then you
must react. When the ball is about to touch
his hands, you must hit the ball, his hands,
or both. Keep the arm that is away from the
ball wrapped around his body. This way if he
does catch it, you can make the tackle.

After the play is done, the key to all
good cornerbacks is having a short memory. If
the play went against you, forget it. There
is always the next one. Remember that mental
and physical preparation and the right
equipment are prerequisites to the process on
the field. Then you have a chance to become
an effective cornerback.

PROFESSIONAL WRITER
Japanese Tea Ceremony

Vance Horne

An American tries to understand a ritual that is totally alien to him in intent and execution. But he knows that in learning about this ceremony he will gain insight into another culture. And he knows that there he will find a reflective experience that he can use in his own life.

1 So Choku Naoko, usually known as Mrs. Gower, is kneeling on a Japanese *tatami* mat in her tea room, trying to tell two West-

erners about tea. The Westerners are kneeling, too, and their knees are hurting. "If on the one hand people stop striving to achieve more, civilization will stop," she says. "But on the other hand, you have to accept yourself as you are." She pauses long enough for the Westerners to quit thinking about their knees and contemplate this unshakeable paradox. "This is what you have to learn," she says, smiling at the dry humor of it.

2   She is dressed in a beautiful kimono and, except for her eyeglasses, there is nothing about her or her tea room to suggest the modern world. This is what she does for a living, showing people how to leave this world briefly through the Japanese tea ceremony. In January she performed parts of the ceremony at The Evergreen State College's Tribute to Japan. I had written a few words telling the public that she would do that. Afterwards she invited me to her Burien home to partake of a full ceremony.

3   I am writing this in the first person because I was one of the two Westerners in the tea room and because I want to confess that the tea ceremony not only impressed me, it baffled me. The centuries-old ceremony is as tidy as algebra but as full of gestures as an opera. It probably is the most Japanese thing there is. Mrs. Gower, a certified teacher, comes from a tea ceremony school in Japan that has 12,000 students, and she estimates that there are 20 to 30 such schools. For years I have heard that if you want to understand Japan, you must understand the tea ceremony.

4   Mrs. Gower's tea room is perhaps 10 feet by 10 feet and a little over 6 feet high. Inside, you see only wood, bamboo, grass mats, rice paper, a sunken pit for a water pot, a small simple chest that holds tea utensils, and a calligraphy scroll. She built the room inside her son's bedroom when he went to college. After years of living in America with her importer/exporter husband, William, she wanted a room that was totally Japanese. It is too small for Westerners to gather in comfortably, but that is part of what the ceremony is about, learning to co-exist. "One-on-one human relationships aren't hard," she says. "But if you have more people, it can become difficult."

5   The ceremony is a way of making a group of people harmonious in a little space, she explains. Basically, it is done by feeding them and giving them tea. She enters the tea room on her knees, bowing. Her guests are against one wall, kneeling, and they must know when they, too, must bow. A girl enters, bear-

ing small but beautiful servings of food in black lacquer serving trays. The guests bow over the food, just as the girl bows. Everyone is in equality, because everyone must know and follow the rituals. Although the girl seems to be a servant, the guests must obey the same rules as she does. Picking up a food bowl, the guests observe the food as if it were a painting. They turn and inspect the bowls in precise gestures. Eating is a dance, and not a simple one. "Tea ceremony has certain unavoidable rules," Mrs. Gower says. "We are living in a do-your-own-thing world. This is totally the reverse."

6   As they finish with a food bowl, the guests take folded paper from their kimonos and wipe the bowl. Then they appreciate its beauty. The girl pours wine in shallow bowls, and the guests drink, but it's not much wine. "Tea ceremony was begun by men," Mrs. Gower explains. "About 100 years ago we had a big cultural revolution in Japan, and men no longer control everything. Today, 95 to 97 percent of the tea industry is controlled by females. Traditionally, the men drank a lot. Now we don't drink so much; we eat instead." She laughs about this turn of events.

7   Everything moves slowly in the ceremony, and it takes a long time to get to the tea part of it. The Japanese relish their time in the tea room. "We are leading a very stressful life," Mrs. Gower says, "and people are trying to escape in many ways. As you walk in a Japanese garden, you leave your stresses behind, and once you enter the tea room you're in a very ideal world. In an ideal world we talk only of pleasant subjects, to make people happy. I am actually leading you to a utopian life. I am leading you to the beauty of life." But such beauty evades the hand or brain that would enclose it. It is the beauty of *u gen*—the unknown. But although the beauty is of the unknown, it isn't necessarily unearthly. In trying to explain it Mrs. Gower even speaks of the beauty of an unknown woman's body beneath her clothes.

8   When Mrs. Gower finally comes to the tea, she carefully opens the chest and takes implements from it. Before she uses them, she inspects them for their beauty, turning them this way and that in a ritual of observation. There is a small ceramic bowl for the tea, a small container holding bright green powdered tea, a simple wood implement that works like a spoon for measuring the tea, a long-handled wooden dipper for getting water from the pot and a curious whisk device for stirring the tea.

9   Her tea room actually is a school room, and she teaches Japanese-Americans the use of these utensils and the rituals of the ceremony as a whole. There are maybe 18 certified teachers in the Seattle area, she thinks, but she has one of only two tea rooms. Actually, she has one American student, a man. The fact that there is but one American makes it clear how Japanese the ceremony is. To learn the ceremony fully usually takes three years.

10   Using her utensils of ancient design, she makes the tea. It is hard to say in words how careful she is. Perhaps it is what one would imagine heart surgery to be. With appropriate bowing on all parts, she serves the tea, and the participants turn the bowls in their hands, admiring them, and at last they drink the bright green and pleasantly bitter tea, and then they clean their bowls.

11   Not much has happened in the physical sense. A simple meal that might take 15 minutes has been drawn out to two hours. Although there is much ritual, there is no invoking of gods, no trading of Zen jests. Mrs. Gower talks of it as a matter of her entertaining guests. "Primarily, entertainment is the love of giving," she says. "Entertainment means nothing if you just call up the caterer. You must give your time and, if I may say it, your compassion."

12   In the end, it is important to see Mrs. Gower as she is. She is not a mysterious and delicate being, conversing only in Buddhistic subtleties. She is an outgoing woman full of humor, and she loves to use American slang. I came away glad to be out of the tea room, because I am not used to such confinement or to such silent ritual or such foreignness. Yet I would like to go back. I am intrigued. A plane ticket to Tokyo and two weeks in a hotel might not take me as close to Japan. In the end, the ceremony reminds me a little of baseball, which is a sport of ritual and of careful geometry, where almost nothing ever happens but it takes a long time. It too is popular in Japan.

EXERCISE 1

1. What is most important in the tea ceremony—the utensils, the food and drink, or the ceremony?

2. What do Japanese people try to escape through the tea ceremony?

3. What in American culture gets in the way of the writer's appreciation?

4. As process analysis, what preparations are made and what is their significance?

5. As process analysis, what are the steps of the Japanese tea ceremony?

PRACTICING PATTERNS OF PROCESS ANALYSIS

█ EXERCISE 2

Refer to the essay "Guarding a Wide Receiver" on page 91. Fill in the blanks to complete the process analysis. Add lines if you need them.

I. Preparation

    A. _____

    B. _____

II. Steps

    A. _____

    B. _____

    C. _____

    D. _____

E. _____

F. _____

G. _____

H. _____

TOPICS FOR ESSAYS OF PROCESS ANALYSIS

Reading-Related Topics

1. "Guarding a Wide Receiver": Use this essay as a model to explain how to perform a particular technique in a team or individual sport. Limit your topic to a function that can be explained in an essay of five to seven paragraphs.
2. "Japanese Tea Ceremony": Write about another ceremony (perhaps religious) in which the consumption of food and/or drink may be less important than the ritual.
3. Write about a toast that is associated with a certain culture, one that is made to health, longevity, relationships, or something else. An example is the Greek custom of breaking wine glasses after a toast on certain occasions.
4. Write about other ceremonies that invite contemplation. For example, Native Americans pass a ceremonial pipe.
5. The Japanese seem to escape from the problems of this world by slowing time and withdrawing. Write about a ceremony different from the Japanese tea ceremony and include comments on the apparent motives (they may not be obvious to most participants) and their fulfillments. If you would like to do some primary research, check your local newspaper for cultural festivals—Armenian, Ukrainian, Greek, Polish, Bohemian, Chinese, Arab, and so on.

Career-Related Topics

6. Explain how to display, package, sell, or demonstrate a product.
7. Explain how to perform a service or to repair or install a product.
8. Explain the procedure for operating a machine, computer, piece of equipment, or other device.
9. Explain how to manufacture or construct something.
10. Explain how to update or modernize a style, product, or concept.

General Topics

Most of the topics below are directive as they are phrased. However, each can be transformed into a "how-it-was-done" informative topic by personalizing it and explaining stage by stage how you, someone else, or a group did something. For example, you could write either a directive process analysis about how to deal with an obnoxious person or an informative process analysis about how you or someone else dealt with an obnoxious person. Keep in mind that the two types of process analysis are often blended, especially in the personal approach. Many of the following topics will be more interesting to you and your readers if they are personalized.

Most of the topics require some narrowing to be treated in an essay. For example, writing about playing baseball is too broad; writing about how to bunt may be manageable.

11. How to end a relationship without hurting someone's feelings

12. How to pass a test for a driver's license

13. How to get a job at _____

14. How to eat _____

15. How to perform a magic trick

16. How to repair _____

17. How to assemble _____

18. How to learn about another culture

19. How to approach someone you would like to know better

20. How to make a videotape of a particular event

WRITER'S GUIDELINES AT A GLANCE: PROCESS ANALYSIS

1. Decide whether your process analysis is mainly directive or informative, and be consistent in using pronouns and other designations.

   - Use second person for the directive as you address the reader (*you, your*).
   - Use first person for the informative; do not address the reader (use *I*); or

- Use third person for the informative; do not address the reader (use *he, she, it, they, them,* individuals, the name of your subject).

2. Consider using this form for the directive process (with topics such as how to cook something or how to fix something).

    I. Preparation
       A.
       B.
       C.
    II. Steps
       A.
       B.
       C.
       D.

3. Consider using this form for the informative process (with topics such as how a volcano functions or how a battle was won).

    I. Background or context
       A.
       B.
       C.
    II. Change or development (narrative)
       A.
       B.
       C.
       D.

4. In explaining the stages and using technical terms, take into account whether your audience will be mainly well informed, moderately informed, or poorly informed.
5. Explain reasons for procedures whenever you believe explanations will help.
6. Use transitional words indicating time or other progression (such as *finally, at last, therefore, consequently,* and—especially for the informative process analysis—words showing passage of time, such as hours, days of the week, and so on).
7. Avoid recipe language; in other words, do not drop *the, a, an,* or *of.*

8

Cause and Effect: Determining Reasons and Results

WRITING ESSAYS OF CAUSE AND EFFECT

Causes and effects deal with reasons and results; they are sometimes discussed together and sometimes separately. Like other forms of writing to explain, writing about causes and effects is based on natural thought processes. The shortest, and arguably the most provocative, poem in the English language—"I/Why?"—is posed by an anonymous author about cause. Children are preoccupied with delightful and often exasperating "why" questions. Daily we encounter all kinds of causes and effects. The same subject may raise questions of both kinds.

> The car won't start. Why? (*cause*)
>
> The car won't start. What now? (*effect*)

At school, from the biology lab to the political science classroom, and at work, from maintaining relationships to changing procedures, causes and effects are found everywhere.

Organizing Cause and Effect

One useful approach to developing a cause-or-effect analysis is *listing*. Write down the event, situation, or trend you are concerned about. Then on the left side, list the causes, and on the right side, list the effects. Here is an example.

103

Causes	Event, Situation, or Trend	Effects
Low self-esteem Drugs Tradition Fear Surrogate family Protection Neighborhood status	Joining a gang	Life of crime Drug addiction Surrogate family relationship Protection Ostracism Restricted vocational opportunities

As you use prewriting techniques to explore your ideas, you need to decide whether your topic should mainly inform or mainly persuade. If you intend to inform, your tone should be coolly objective. If you intend to persuade, your tone should be subjective. In either case, you should take into account the views of your audience as you phrase your ideas. You should also take into account how much your audience understands about your topic and develop your ideas accordingly.

Composing the Thesis

Now that you have organized your ideas under causes and effects, you are ready to focus on the causes, on the effects, or, occasionally, on both.

Your controlling idea or thesis might be one of causes: "People join gangs for three main reasons." Later, as you use the idea as a thesis in an essay, you would rephrase it to make it less mechanical, allowing it to become part of the flow of your discussion. If you wanted to personalize the work—thereby probably making it more interesting—you could write about someone you know who joined a gang. And you could use the same basic framework, the three causes, to indicate why this particular person joined a gang.

Your selection of a thesis takes you to the next writing phase: that of completing an outline or outline alternative. There you need to consider three closely related points:

- Considering kinds of causes and effects
- Evaluating the importance of sequence
- Introducing ideas and working with patterns

Considering Kinds of Causes and Effects

Causes and effects can be primary or secondary, immediate or remote.

Primary or Secondary

Primary means "major," and *secondary* means "minor." A primary cause may be sufficient to bring about the situation (subject). For example, infidelity may be a primary (and possibly sufficient by itself) cause of divorce for some people but not for others, who regard it as secondary. Or if country X is attacked by country Y, the attack itself, as a primary cause, may be sufficient to bring on a declaration of war. But a diplomatic blunder regarding visas for workers may be of secondary importance, and though significant, it is certainly not enough to start a war over.

Immediate or Remote

Causes and effects often occur at a distance in time or place from the situation. The immediate effect of sulfur in the atmosphere may be atmospheric pollution, but the long-range, or remote, effect may be acid rain and the loss of species. The immediate cause of the greenhouse effect may be the depletion of the ozone layer, whereas the long-range, or remote, cause is the use of CFCs (commonly called Freons, which are found in such items as Styrofoam cups). Even more remote, the ultimate cause may be the people who use the products containing Freons. Your purpose will determine the causes and effects appropriate for your essay.

Evaluating the Importance of Sequence

The sequence in which events occur(red) may or may not be significant. When you are dealing with several sequential events, determine whether the sequence of events has causal connections; that is, does one cause bring about another?

Consider this sequence of events: Joe's parents get divorced, and Joe joins a gang. We know that one reason for joining a gang is to gain family companionship. Therefore, we may conclude that Joe joined the gang in order to satisfy his needs for family companionship, which he lost when his parents were divorced. But if we do so, we may have reached a wrong conclusion, because Joe's joining the gang after the family breakup does not necessarily mean that the two events are related. Maybe Joe joined the gang because of drug dependency, low self-esteem, or a need for protection.

In each case, examine the connections. To assume that one event is *caused* by another just because it *follows* the other is a logical error called a *post hoc* ("after this") fallacy. An economic depression may occur after a president takes office, but that does not necessarily mean the depression was caused by the new administration. It might have occurred anyway, perhaps in an even more severe form.

Order

The order of the causes and effects you discuss in your paper may be based on time, space, emphasis, or a combination:

- *Time*: If one stage leads to another, as in a discussion of the causes and effects of upper atmospheric pollution, your paper would be organized best by time.
- *Space:* In some instances causes and effects are best organized by their relation in space. For instance, the causes of an economic recession could be discussed in terms of local factors, regional factors, national factors, and international factors.
- *Emphasis:* Some causes and effects may be more important than others. For instance, if some causes of divorce are primary (perhaps infidelity and physical abuse) and others are secondary (such as annoying habits and laziness), a paper about divorce could present the secondary causes first, and then move on to primary causes to emphasize the latter as more important.

In some instances, two or more factors (such as time and emphasis) may be linked; in that case, select the order that best fits what you are trying to say, or combine orders.

Introducing Ideas and Working with Patterns

In introducing your controlling idea—probably in an introductory paragraph—you will almost certainly want to perform two functions:

1. *Discuss your subject.* For example, if you are writing about the causes or effects of divorce, begin with a statement about divorce as a subject.
2. *Indicate whether you will concentrate on causes or effects or combine them.* That indication should be made clear early in the paper. Concentrating on one—causes or effects—does not mean you will not mention the other; it only means you will

emphasize one of them. You can lend emphasis to your main concern(s), causes, or effects, or a combination, by repeating key words such as *cause, reason, effect, result, consequence,* and *outcome.*

The most likely pattern for your work is shown below.

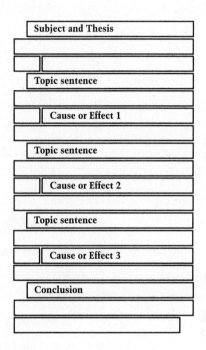

EXAMINING ESSAYS OF CAUSE AND EFFECT

Student Writer

What If I'm Overweight and Not Jolly?

Karen Peterson

Working with the basic idea of identifying with those with different experiences, student Karen Peterson asks you to walk in her shoes. Peterson is a hardworking, highly competent, witty student. She says that she has experienced all of the things you are going to read about, but now she has accepted herself for what she is—a proud and beautiful woman with a lot of confidence, intelligence, sensitivity, and self-fulfillment, who happens to be overweight.

Thesis   Society as a whole views being fat as unacceptable. <u>This stereotype has devastating psychological effects</u>. People are taught to believe that those who are fat are unhealthy, unhappy, low in self-esteem, unmotivated, and lazy.

Having none of those characteristics, I say society is really misjudging people. I am overweight, but I do not fit the stereotype. I am in great health. I am subject to the same emotions as those of a thin person. As far as having low self-esteem, for me that couldn't be farther from the truth. I have always liked myself and have been secure in who I am. With regard to being unmotivated and lazy, I go to school full-time (17 semester units), and I take care of a household of four. In my opinion, I make the White Tornado look sluggish by comparison.

Cause   <u>The fashion industry, which is also dictated to by society, has long ignored the "full figure."</u> When I was growing up, it was difficult to find fashionable, stylish clothing that fit me. Most clothing manufacturers designed clothes for the "model" figure, even though the world's population isn't all models. I often found myself going from store to store, discovering

	that the only place that carried my size was
Effect	something like Coleman Tents R Us. <u>This may</u>
	<u>seem funny, but for a person like me, it can</u>
	<u>be traumatic.</u>

Cause   <u>The media contribute to stereotyping by</u> <u>promoting the idea that in order to be</u> <u>beautiful, happy, healthy, and loved, a person</u> <u>must be thin.</u> They promote this concept by showing thin people exclusively when they advertise cosmetics, clothing, cards, and alcohol. Only thin people are seen enjoying

Effect   themselves on vacations. <u>It's no wonder that</u> <u>fat people feel overwhelmed and defeated, when</u> <u>this is the image they continually see on</u> <u>virtually every television commercial,</u> <u>billboard, magazine cover, and movie.</u> These concepts and images create extreme pressure to

Effect
(example)   conform. For instance, <u>Oprah Winfrey was</u> <u>subjected to pressure and ridicule when one</u> <u>diet didn't work.</u> She failed to fit the media's image. But she was still the same person. Surely a person is worth more than an image, heavy or light. Like her, I'm worth more than a perfect image.

Cause   <u>The worst offender of social stereotyping</u> <u>of fat people is the health-and-fitness</u> <u>industry.</u> No other industry can do more psychological and physical damage while

making a bundle of money by exploiting fat
people. With all the fad diets, quick-weight-
loss pills, "miracle" fat creams, and
exercise weight-loss videos, it is no wonder
that fat people don't know whom to believe,
which weight-loss guru to follow, or simply
how to lose weight successfully and safely.
All of the marketed diets and solutions seem
to place great emphasis on being fit and
healthy. Yet in reality, many are
detrimental. For most of my life, I have
tried a variety of these so-called get-thin-
quick regimens. The outcome at first was
always great, but they fail to help me

Effect maintain the new, thin look. What resulted is
commonly known as the yo-yo syndrome. I lost
weight, but once I stopped dieting, the old
habit and pounds returned, sometimes
accompanied by even more pounds.

Reflection on People really need to accept others for
thesis the way they are and not put so much emphasis
on how they look. Stereotyping of any form
is, to say the least, demeaning—mentally,
physically, and spiritually. To assume that
an individual is any less of a human being
because of his or her weight is pure
ignorance. It tends to get in the way of good
friendships, relationships, communication,

understanding, and compassion. A human being
is a human being regardless of size.

PROFESSIONAL WRITER

La Vida Loca: Crazy Life, Crazy Death

Carlos A. Chavez and Antonio H. Rodriguez

How can we be hopeful for young men whose lives are marginalized by the fatalistic mentality of barrio warfare? Carlos A. Chavez, director of community and public relations at Occidental College, and Antonio H. Rodriguez, civil rights attorney, search for hope and solutions in the midst of chaos.

1   For the last week we've held vigil over Jaramillo Rodriguez, our 19-year-old nephew. His body lies inert, invaded by tubes and tethered to electronic machines that do the basic biological work that this strapping, 6-foot-4 boy is currently incapable of sustaining. Once a promising athlete, he lies near death, another young victim to the brutal gang warfare plaguing the City of Angels.

2   He and his two "homies" were cut down by gunfire from rival gang members over disputes that are totally baffling even to those familiar with the self-destructive lifestyle called *la vida loca*, the crazy life. It's irrelevant whether the dispute was over control of territory (usually involving short stretches of bleak barrio asphalt), or personal insult (perceived as violating the integrity of an exaggerated sense of pride and honor) or simply the chance encounter by rival members of kamikaze-like youth gangs.

3   What is shocking is the degree to which this formerly romanticized rite-of-passage lifestyle has degenerated into a self-destructive, alienated, fatalistic ideology that holds sway over so many of our children. Spawned by the fraying fabric of barrio life and fueled by popular culture's steady diet of conflict resolution through violence, this view of life as mayhem is causing too many of our intelligent, eager school-age kids to mutate into teen warriors without a cause.

4   During the early part of the Chicano power movement in the late '60s, the *vato loco* (crazy guy) was cast as the embodiment of resistance to sinister cultural aggression. His unconventional clothing, colorful *caló* dialect—a unique blend of Spanish and English—and insolent demeanor made him the definition of "cool" in the barrio. Chicano college student activists adopted

the cool look: white T-shirts under plaid Pendelton wool shirts with a military press and sharply creased khakis or jeans.

5   But in those days, most *vatos* became *veteranos* by their 20s and outgrew the crazy life. Some led a dual life, going to school or work during the week and hanging out in the neighborhood on weekends. Guns were a rare commodity and drive-bys were just beginning to be used as a gang tactic. Most *veteranos* made the transition to the work force as semiskilled and skilled laborers and as professionals. While Los Angeles was just as segregated and racist a city as it is now, there were job opportunities and the evidence for believing in the future was found on every Eastside street: Guys working for a living as did their fathers and grandfathers before them.

6   The loss of blue-collar jobs, combined with the curtailment of social spending, has eroded employment and educational opportunities for our children to the point that they are extremely marginalized. In the process, the adolescent lifestyle for many of them appears to have become a life sentence.

7   Barrio life for most gang youths is marked by self-destructive activity often terminated by incarceration or death. Confronted by armed gangsters on one side and police on the other, a homie's life is dictated by a live-for-today attitude in which the goal is to stay alive by warding off attacks and inflicting attacks on rivals without getting arrested. Behind bars, the mayhem and, often, killing continue.

8   These children have no hope. For them, fatalism has replaced faith. At the hospital this week, one of our nephew's friends commented on the tragedy: "It's messed up, hey, but everybody has to go some day. I know it may happen to me. But that's all right. I'll die for my barrio." The young man was no older than 15, but he already presented a chilling and disheartening combination of attitudes: childlike idealism and a reckless disregard for human life.

9   The gang mentality alienates these youths from their families and from the community. Their mind-set has them in a constant battlefield superconsciousness, like soldiers in battle, that numbs them to the sensitivities and the needs of others. When they grieve for their fallen friends, a frequent occurrence, they do so profoundly, intensely, but only for a very brief period—they must remain hypervigilant and combat ready in the low-intensity warfare their lives have become. To relax or drop your guard could mean death.

10   As we wrestle with the pain, the remorse and self-reproach about how we could have done more to prevent the tragedy, the deadly hold that gang life has is haunting us. Our nephew and his friend were hit after they had made a commitment to bail out of the gang-banger life. Our nephew had begun to make arrangements to move out of Southern California. His friend, also on life support, had gone back to night school to earn a diploma and qualify for the armed forces. He had about one month to go. (The other friend has recovered from his wounds.)

11   Where can we find hope in the future when young men like this see none for themselves? Our family's tragedy is but one of many in this city. And like so many other families, we continue our vigil for a young man on life support, with a hope born in an earlier era.

EXERCISE 1

1. How do the writers of *"La Vida Loca"* characterize the attitudes of the gang members (paragraph 3)?

2. What do the authors say are the causes of this self-destructive behavior?

3. What is the difference between the gang members now and the *vatos loco* of the '60s?

4. What social changes affected the outlets for rebellious youth?

5. What is the homie's "live-for-today" attitude?

6. Why do the gang members say they will die for their barrios?

7. Are gang members supported by their communities and families?

8. Do the authors have a solution? Do you?

PRACTICING PATTERNS OF CAUSE AND EFFECT

EXERCISE 2

Fill in the blanks to complete first the causes outline and then the effects outline.

1. Causes for dropping out of high school

   I. Family tradition

   II. _____

   III. _____

   IV. _____

2. Effects of getting a college education

   I. Better informed

   II. _____

   III. _____

   IV. _____

TOPICS FOR ESSAYS OF CAUSE AND EFFECT

Reading-Related Topics

1. "What If I'm Overweight and Not Jolly?": Peterson objects to being discriminated against. Write an essay of cause and/or effect about another group of people who are discriminated against.
2. "*La Vida Loca:* Crazy Life, Crazy Death": In an essay of cause and/or effect, write about someone you know who became a gang member.
3. Write a cause and effect essay about addiction as a form of "crazy life, crazy death."

Career-Related Topics

4. Discuss the effects (benefits) of a particular product or service on the business community, family life, society generally, a specific group (age, income, interest), or an individual.
5. Discuss the needs (thus the cause of development) by individuals, families, or institutions for a particular product or type of product.
6. Discuss the effects of using a certain approach or philosophy in sales, personnel management, or customer service.

General Topics

Regard each of the listed items as a subject (situation, circumstance, or trend) that has causes and effects. Then determine whether you will concentrate on causes, effects, or a combination. You can probably write a more interesting, well-developed, and therefore successful essay on a topic you can personalize. For example, a discussion about a specific young person who contemplated, attempted, or committed suicide is probably a better topic idea than a general discussion of suicide. If you do not personalize the topic, you will probably have to do some basic research to supply details for development.

7. Attending or completing college
8. Having or getting a job
9. Change in policy or administration
10. Change in coaches, teachers, officeholder(s)
11. Alcoholism
12. Gambling
13. Moving to another country, state, or home
14. Exercise
15. Passing or failing a test or course
16. Popularity of a certain TV program or song
17. Early marriage
18. Teenage parenthood

WRITER'S GUIDELINES AT A GLANCE: CAUSE AND EFFECT

1. Determine whether your topic should mainly inform or mainly persuade, and use the right tone for your purpose and audience.
2. Use listing to brainstorm cause-and-effect ideas. This is a useful form:

Causes	Event, Situation, or Trend	Effects
1.	—	1.
2.	—	2.
3.	—	3.
4.	—	4.

3. Decide whether to concentrate on causes, effects, or a combination of causes and effects. Many short essays will discuss causes and effects but use one as the framework for the piece. A typical basic outline might look like this:

   Thesis:

      I. Cause or Effect 1
     II. Cause or Effect 2
    III. Cause or Effect 3

4. Do not conclude that something is an effect merely because it follows something else.
5. Lend emphasis to your main concern(s), causes or effects, or a combination, by repeating key words, such as *cause, reason, effect, result, consequence,* and *outcome.*
6. Causes and effects can be primary or secondary, immediate or remote.
7. The order of causes and effects in your paper may be based on time, space, emphasis, or a combination.

9

Classification: Establishing Groups

Writing Essays of Classification

To explain by classification, you put persons, places, things, or ideas into groups or classes based on their characteristics. Whereas analysis by division deals with the characteristics of just one unit, classification deals with more than one unit, so the subject is plural.

To classify efficiently, try following this procedure:

1. Select a plural subject.
2. Decide on a principle for grouping the units of your subject.
3. Establish the groups, or classes.
4. Write about the classes.

Selecting a Subject

When you say you have different kinds of neighbors, friends, teachers, bosses, or interests, you are classifying; that is, you are forming groups.

In naming the different kinds of people in your neighborhood, you might think of different groupings of your neighbors, the units. For example, some neighbors are friendly, some are meddlesome, and some are private. Some neighbors have yards like Japanese gardens, some have yards like neat but cozy parks, and some have yards like abandoned lots. Some neighbors are affluent, some are comfortable, and some are struggling. Each of these sets is a classification system and could be the focus of one paragraph in your essay.

Using a Principle to Avoid Overlapping

All the sets in the preceding section are sound because each group is based on a single concern: neighborly involvement, appearance of the yard, or wealth. This one concern, or controlling idea, is called the *principle*. For example, the principle of neighborly involvement controls the grouping of neighbors into three classes: friendly, meddlesome, and private.

All the classes in any one group must adhere to the controlling principle for that group. You would not say, for example, that your neighbors can be classified as friendly, meddlesome, private, and affluent, because the first three classes relate to neighborly involvement, but the fourth, relating to wealth, refers to another principle. Any one of the first three—the friendly, meddlesome, and private— might also be affluent. The classes should not overlap in this way. Also, every member should fit into one of the available classes.

Establishing Classes

As you name your classes, rule out easy, unimaginative phrasing such as *fast/medium/slow*, *good/average/bad*, and *beautiful/ordinary/ugly*. Look for creative, original phrases and unusual perspectives.

> *Subject:* neighbors
> *Principle*: neighborhood involvement
> *Classes*: friendly, meddlesome, private

> *Subject*: neighbors
> *Principle*: yard upkeep
> *Classes:* immaculate, neat, messy

> *Subject*: neighbors
> *Principle:* wealth
> *Classes*: affluent, comfortable, struggling

Using Simple and Complex Forms

Classification can take two forms: simple and complex. The *simple* form does not go beyond main divisions in its groupings.

> *Subject*: Neighbors
> *Principle*: Involvement
> *Classes*: I. Friendly
>   II. Meddlesome
>   III. Private

Complex classifications are based on one principle and then subgrouped by another related principle. The following example classifies neighbors by their neighborly involvement. It then subgroups two of the classes on the basis of motive.

I. Friendly
II. Meddlesome
    A. Controlling
    B. Emotionally needy

III. Private
    A. Shy
    B. Snobbish
    C. Secretive

EXAMINING ESSAYS OF CLASSIFICATION

Student Writer

Types of Hepatitis

Annie Chen

While volunteering to donate blood, Annie Chen discovered that she had hepatitis. After going to the doctor, she went to the library in search of medical information. Propelling her was one of the strongest motives she had ever had for doing research: concern about her health. She soon became a lay "expert" and was able to write about the different kinds of hepatitis.

Two years ago when I stopped at a hospital to donate blood, a simple screening procedure determined that I had hepatitis, a disease that involves the inflammation of the liver. After going to my doctor, who gave me information, instructions, and a shot of gamma globulin, I immediately went to the library. Nothing could stop me from learning what I could about this disease I thought only other people had. What I found there confirmed in more detail what the doctor had

Subject   told me. Hepatitis has distinct symptoms:

jaundice, vomiting, nausea, poor appetite,

Principle and general weakness. Nevertheless, <u>hepatitis</u>

is not a single disease coming from the same

Principle source; instead <u>it mainly takes three</u>

<u>different forms, which are known as type A,</u>

Thesis <u>type B, and type C.</u>

Topic   <u>Hepatitis A is the seventh most commonly</u>
sentence
Class 1 <u>reported infectious disease in the United</u>

<u>States</u> (behind gonorrhea, chicken pox,

syphilis, AIDS, salmonellosis, and

shigellosis). Type A hepatitis is highly

contagious and is commonly transmitted by

human waste. It is also acquired by the

ingestion of contaminated food, milk, or

water; therefore, this type is said to be

toxic. Outbreaks of this type are often

traced to eating seafood from polluted water.

The highest incidence of hepatitis A is in

children, about thirty percent of them younger

than fifteen. Fortunately, when treated with

medicines such as gamma globulin, symptoms are

gone in less than six weeks.

Topic   <u>Unlike hepatitis A, hepatitis B is caused</u>
sentence
Class 2 <u>by a virus</u>. Though it can also be transmitted

by contact with human secretions and feces,

it is most frequently spread during intimate

sexual contact and the sharing of needles by

drug abusers. Nurses, doctors, laboratory

technicians, and dentists are often exposed to type B hepatitis. A common infectious disease in Southeast Asian countries, hepatitis B is much more serious than A. Although most patients recover completely, some with weak immune systems may carry the virus for more than a year and may become chronic carriers.

Topic sentence Class 3   <u>In 1990 the hepatitis C virus was identified</u>. It is spread by blood-to-blood contact. Therefore, any way that one person's blood may be in contact with an infected person's blood will spread the hepatitis C virus. Some of the most common means of transmission are blood transfusions, intravenous drug use, tattooing, body piercing, and sharing needles. Type C now accounts for about twenty percent of all viral hepatitis cases.

In most hepatitis patients, the liver cells will eventually regenerate with little or no residual damage. I feel perfectly fine, and there are no worries for other patients like me. Although hepatitis is an extremely troublesome disease, blood screening for transfusions, effective medicines, and good health practices have minimized the effects, at least for the informed and careful public.

PROFESSIONAL WRITER

Why We Carp and Harp

Mary Ann Hogan

Nag, Nag, Nag, Stop! Stop! Stop! We know nagging, don't we? After all, we've heard so much of it that we're experts, right? Maybe not. Listen to what this expert says about types of naggers. She points out that in this sophisticated world, some people specialize in certain kinds of nagging.

1 Bring those dishes down from your room! Put those scissors away. . . . I told you not to smoke in the kitchen and you shouldn't be smoking anyway! Take your feet off the table! Why do I have to tell you again and again . . .?! The hills are alive with the sound of nagging—the gnawing, crescendoing timbre of people getting in each other's face. Parents nag children, wives nag husbands, husbands nag wives, friends nag friends . . . "*Use* your fork . . . *Stop* spending money like water . . . *Can't* you be ready on time? . . . *Act* like an adult . . . ." Nagging, of course, has been around since the first cave husband refused to take out the cave garbage. But linguists, psychologists and other scholars are just now piecing together what nagging really is, why we do it, and how to stop it before we nag each other to death.

2 Common perception holds that a nag is an unreasonably demanding wife who carps at a long-suffering husband. But in truth, nagging is universal. It happens in romances, in families, in businesses, in society—wherever people gather and one person wants another to do something he or she doesn't want to do. "It's a virus. You pick it up through kissing, shaking hands and standing in crowded rooms with people who have perfect children, wonderful husbands and sterlized homes," says humor columnist Erma Bombeck, whose family members nag her as artfully as she nags them. "It makes you feel good—like you're getting something done. Most of us want perfection in this world," she adds.

3 Thus, doctors can nag patients to lose their potbellies; accountants can nag timid clients to buy low; bosses can nag workers to get things done on time; special interest groups can nag the public to save the planet and send money, and the government can nag everyone to pay their taxes on time, to abstain from drink if they're pregnant and, while they're at it, to Buy American. And when the going gets desperate, the desperate get

nagging: Our recession-plagued nation, experts say, could be headed for a giant nag jag.

4   "When people are generally dissatisfied, they tend to harp at other people more," says Bernard Zilbergeld, a Bay Area psychologist. Naggers tend to fall into four categories—friendly, professional, social and domestic—that range from the socially acceptable to the toxic.

5   The Friendly Ones are proud of their art. "My sisters call me a nag, but that's not necessarily a bad thing," says Bari Brenner, a 44-year-old Castro Valley resident who describes herself as "a third-generation nag" with a low tolerance for procrastinators. "I get things done. The truth is I'm organized, they're not. I can see the big *picture*. They can't. We're going on a trip to England. 'Did you call the travel agent?' 'No.' 'Well, *call* the travel agent . . . book the hotel . . . call *now*!' It's the same thing at work. Nagging can be a means to an end."

6   Professional Nags—people who do it for a living—have to disguise what they do to get what they want. "I have to nag all the time—but you have to be careful about using the word *nag*," says Ruth Holton, a lobbyist for Common Cause, the good-government advocacy group. "I have to ask [legislators] for the same thing over and over again, year in, year out. But if they perceive what you're doing as nagging, they'll say, 'I've heard this 100 times before,' and they'll shut down. There's a fine line between artful persistence and being perceived as a nag."

7   Social nags don't see themselves as naggers. The U.S. Surgeon General's office peppers us with health warnings and calls it education. Environmentalists harp on people to recycle and save the rain forest, all in the name of the Greater Good. "One person's nagger is another person trying to save the world," says Arthur Asa Berger, a popular culture critic at San Francisco State University.

8   Then, somewhere beyond the limits of social convention, lies the dangerous world of the good old-fashioned Domestic Nag. Observers of the human condition, from the Roman poets to the purveyors of prime-time TV, have mined domestic nagging's quirkiness for laughs. But behavioral experts say that's where nagging can run amok. At best, domestic nagging is irritating. In Neil Simon's *The Odd Couple*, Felix wanted Oscar to clean up his act. Oscar liked being a slob. Felix nagged, nothing changed, and Felix finally moved out. At its worst, domestic nagging is murderous. In England last May, a 44-year-old busi-

nessman strangled his wife after 15 years of her nagging finally made him snap. In January, a judge ruled that the wife's verbal abuse justifiably provoked him and gave the husband an 18-month suspended sentence.

9   What causes this dynamic of domestic demolition? At the root of nagging, behavioralists say, lies a battle for control. It begins with a legitimate request: "I need you to hear me . . . to be with me . . . to be around, to do things like take out the garbage." But the person being asked doesn't want to change and sees the request as a threat to his or her control of the status quo. So the request is ignored.

10   "From the nagger's point of view, the naggee isn't listening," says Andrew Christensen, a UCLA psychology professor who has studied nagging for four years. "From there, it escalates. The further you withdraw, the more I nag. The naggee's point of view is, 'If I don't respond, maybe you'll shut up.'" The original request gets lost in the power struggle. The nagging takes on a life of its own. The desperate refrain of "Take out the garbage!" can stand for a whole universe of complaints, from "You never do anything around here" to "I hate your stupid brown shoes!" "Sometimes I go through the house saying, 'Dammit, close the cupboards! Don't leave the towels on the floor! What's so hard about moving a vacuum cleaner across the hall. . . .' Bang! Bang! Bang! The list goes on," says a 40-year-old Mill Valley mother of two schoolchildren. "It's like the tape is stuck on replay and nobody's listening."

11   UCLA's Christensen calls it the "demand-withdraw pattern." In 60% of the couples he's studied, women were in the demanding, or nagging, role. In 30% of the cases, men were the demanders. In 10%, the roles were equal. "It may be that, traditionally, women have been more interested in closeness and sharing feelings, and men have been more interested in privacy," he says.

12   The scenario of the man coming home from work and the woman spending the day with the kids feeds the gender stereotype of the female nag. "He wants to sit in front of the TV, she's primed to have an empathetic listener," Christensen says. "The reverse is true with sex. There, men tend to be in the nagging role. Either way, one feels abandoned, neglected and deprived, the other feels intruded upon. It's a stalemate."

13   Communications experts say there is a way to end the nagging. Both people have the power to stop. What it takes is

earnest willingness to step out of the ritual. The naggee could say: "You keep bringing up the issue of the garbage. I'd like to sit down and talk about it." But the gesture would have to be heartfelt, not an exercise in lip service. The nagger could write a note instead of carping. "People tend to react differently to written communication," says Zilbergeld. In either case, the effect is paradoxical: When the nagger stops, it leaves room for the naggee to act. When the naggee listens, there's nothing to nag about.

14   And if it doesn't stop? "It gets more and more robotic," says Gahan Wilson, the *New Yorker* magazine artist who explored the fate of the Nag Eternal in a recent cartoon. "We spend much of our lives on automatic pilot."

EXERCISE 1

1. What is being classified in Hogan's essay?

2. What is the classification based on?

3. Where is the thesis stated?

4. Translate the basic parts of the classification into a simple topic outline.

    I. Friendly   II. Professional
       A.   A.
       B.   B.

III. Social   IV. Domestic
   A.   A.
   B.   B.

5. What do the behavioralists say is at the root of nagging?

6. How does the idea of control relate to each of the four groups of naggers?

7. How do you react to nagging from family and close friends?

8. Do some people like to be nagged and even depend on naggers for direction?

PRACTICING PATTERNS OF CLASSIFICATION

EXERCISE 2

Fill in the blanks to identify classes that could be discussed for each subject.

1. Subjects: Professional athletes
   Principle: Why they participate in sports
   Classes:

   I. Glory

   II. _____

   III. _____

2. Subjects: Pet owners
   Principle: Why they own (need) pets
   Classes:

   I. Companionship

   II. _____

   III. _____

TOPICS FOR ESSAYS OF CLASSIFICATION

Reading-Related Topics

1. "Types of Hepatitis": Write an essay in which you discuss the various types of another disease, such as diabetes, skin cancer, arthritis, herpes, pneumonia, leukemia, or lupus. Some of these diseases not only have classes but subclasses as well. Medical books and encyclopedias can provide you with basic information.
2. "Why We Carp and Harp": Pick one of the classes of naggers (such as domestic), and show in an essay how the category can be divided into subclasses.
3. Write an essay in which you classify those who are nagged (the naggees).
4. Using Hogan's set of classes as a framework, discuss each kind of nagger with examples from your experience and your reading.

Career-Related Topics

5. Discuss the different types of managers you have encountered (democratic, authoratarian, authoritative, autocratic, buddy-like, aloof).
6. Discuss the different types of customers with whom you have dealt (perhaps according to their purpose for seeking your services or products).
7. Discuss the different types of employees you have observed.
8. Discuss the different qualities of products or services in a particular field.

General Topics

Select one of the following groups and then decide on a principle for classifying the members. For example, *smiles* might be grouped according to reasons for smiling.

9. Laundromat users
10. Summer jobs
11. People who exercise
12. Ways of disciplining children
13. Diets
14. Dreams
15. Trucks
16. Drivers
17. Sports announcers
18. Mothers or fathers
19. Neighbors
20. Police officers
21. Clergy
22. Pet owners
23. Music
24. Parks
25. Smiles

WRITER'S GUIDELINES AT A GLANCE: CLASSIFICATION

1. Follow this procedure for writing essays of classification:

   - Select a plural subject.
   - Decide on a principle for grouping the units of your subject.
   - Establish the groups, or classes.
   - Write about the classes.

2. Avoid uninteresting phrases for your classes, such as *good/average/bad, fast/medium/slow,* and *beautiful/ordinary/ugly.*
3. Avoid overlapping classes.
4. The Roman numeral parts of your outline will probably indicate your classes.

   I. Class one
   II. Class two
   III. Class three

5. If you use subclasses, clearly indicate the different levels.
6. Following your outline or outline alternative, give somewhat equal (however much is appropriate) space to each class.

10

Comparison and Contrast: Showing Similarities and Differences

WRITING ESSAYS OF COMPARISON AND CONTRAST

Comparison and contrast is a method of showing similarities and dissimilarities between subjects. *Comparison* is concerned with organizing and developing points of similarity; *contrast* has the same function for dissimilarity. In some instances a writing assignment may require that you cover only similarities or only dissimilarities. Occasionally, an instructor may ask you to separate one from the other. Usually, you will combine them within the larger design of your essay. For convenience, the term *comparison* is often applied to both comparison and contrast, because both use the same techniques and are usually combined into one operation.

This chapter will help you deal with topics and choose strategies in writing comparison and contrast.

Generating Topics and Working with the 4 P's

Comparison and contrast is basic to your thinking. In your daily activities, you consider similarities and dissimilarities among persons, things, concepts, political leaders, doctors, friends, instructors, schools, nations, classes, movies, and so on. You naturally turn to comparison and contrast to solve problems and to make decisions in your actions and in your writing. Because you have had so many comparative experiences, finding a topic to write about is likely to be only a matter of choosing from a great number of appealing ideas. Freewriting, brainstorming, and clustering will help you generate topics that are especially workable and appropriate for particular essay assignments.

130

Many college writing assignments will specify a topic or ask you to choose one from a list. Regardless of the source of your topic, the procedure for developing your ideas by comparison and contrast is the same as the procedure for developing topics of your own choosing. That procedure can be appropriately called the "4 P's": *purpose, points, patterns,* and *presentation.*

Purpose

Are you trying to show relationships (how things are similar and dissimilar) or to prove that one side is better (ranking)?

Let's say you have heard a great deal of discussion about different generations, especially the Baby Boomers and Generation X. Although you could argue that one generation is better than the other, in your quest for understanding, you probably would choose to emphasize relationships. That choice would become a thesis such as this: Although similar in certain ways, the Baby Boomers and Generation X are significantly different.

Points

Next you might brainstorm a list of ideas that could be applied somewhat equally to the two subjects, Baby Boomers and Generation X. From the list, you would decide which points have the most potential for discussion. Here is such a list; the most promising points are circled.

attitudes toward family (having children, getting married)
music
philosophy (especially optimistic and pessimistic tendencies)
fashion
materialism
education (both having and wanting)
religion
attitudes toward careers

Pattern

Then you should decide on the better way to organize your material: subject by subject or point by point. You would use the same information in each pattern, but the organization would be different.

The *subject-by-subject* pattern presents all of one side and then all of the other.

I. Baby Boomers
   A. Attitude toward careers
   B. Attitude toward family
   C. Materialism
II. Generation X
   A. Attitude toward careers
   B. Attitude toward family
   C. Materialism

The *point-by-point* pattern shows one point in relation to the sides (subjects) one at a time. This is the more common pattern.

I. Attitude toward careers
   A. Baby Boomers
      1. Details, examples, explanations
      2. Details, examples, explanations
   B. Generation X
      1. Details, examples, explanations
      2. Details, examples, explanations
II. Attitude toward family (same specific support as above)
   A. Baby Boomers
   B. Generation X
III. Materialism (same specific support as above)
   A. Baby Boomers
   B. Generation X

Presentation

Then, you would use your outline (or cluster list), to begin writing your essay. The Roman numerals in the outline usually indicate topic sentences, and therefore paragraphs. The Arabic numerals (details, examples, explanations) become more specific support.

EXAMINING ESSAYS OF COMPARISON AND CONTRAST

Student Writer

Families: Street and Prison

Jodie Monroe

Having experienced two kinds of families, one as she grew up and the other after she was incarcerated, Jodie Monroe had firsthand experience to write about. In this essay she is, of course, not concerned about which is better; instead, she focuses on the remarkable similarities of two types of families—street and prison.

Thesis

When I say that all parts of ordinary society also exist in a women's prison, people sometimes say, "What about families?" The answer is easy. Yes, even families. And prison families even have all the parts that "street" families do. Although most inmates are not and will not be involved in prison families, I've been in two, and I've observed dozens of them from up close. I know all about the parents, the children and relatives, and the activities. I even know about the broken families.

Topic sentence

I. Leaders

A. Street

A. Prison

Whether the family is conventional or prison, the parents set the tone. In conventional families, it's the male and female partners we associate with television sitcom couples: Ward and June Cleaver, Cliff and Claire Huxtable, Roseanne and Dan Conners. The parents hold things together and solve problems. In prison, it's a strong lesbian couple that attracts a family arrangement. Usually one member has the masculine image and the other has the feminine. Sometimes the authority is shared, but as with TV families, the male figure is usually dominant. One family in our unit now has a dominant father figure called "Daddy Wabash" (who likes to play "Wabash Cannonball" on her harmonica), and "Mama Catalina" (who frequently wears a bathing suit for underwear).

Topic Sentence

II. Offspring

A. Street

Offspring have their family needs, regardless of where they are. In conventional families, kids are busy growing up. They want to be independent, but they want their comforts and nurturing. They need guidance and protection, even from themselves. Wherever they are, families also enjoy the sense of having an extended family with aunts, uncles, cousins, and grandparents. The

B. Prison

prison "children" are the same in almost all respects. They want the security they once had in a family or simply the security that others had and they didn't when they were growing up in dysfunctional families, foster homes, and juvenile halls. Cricket and Loco are two such prison children. It so happens that they are young and both products of foster homes and juvenile halls, but not all prison children are young; they just need to be willing subordinates to a couple in a family arrangement. Cricket and Loco are not sexually involved with anyone, but that can vary, too. Daddy Wabash and Mama Catalina

boss their children around, but they also
protect them from some of the strong-arming
that goes on out on the yard, and they
provide them with birthday parties, family
conferences, and special family meals and
get-togethers. The extended family is likely
to have some cousins, aunts and uncles, and
sometimes grandparents who will attend
meetings periodically and be around to
satisfy their own special needs and provide
services. In return, children such as Cricket
and Loco clean their parents' cells and bring
them special presents. This being summer, one
will sometimes see Cricket and Loco bring ice
water to the family meetings and use swatters
to keep flies away from their parents. People
are commonly called "Mama" and "Daddy" and
"Daughter" and so on. Sometimes drugs and
prison wine (called "hootch") are part of
family life.

Topic Sentence

III. Breakups

A. Street

B. Prison

These days families everywhere break up
in record number. More than half the regular
marriages will end in divorce. When that
occurs the family may be divided and members
will join other families. The prison
situation is not so different. The parent
couple, such as Daddy Wabash and Mama
Catalina, may break up (over drugs,

infidelity, or basic incompatibility), one
parent may get sent to a different prison, or
one parent may be paroled. When that occurs,
the remaining parent may take on a new
partner, even someone else from the family,
and the family will continue. Or the family
may just disintegrate. The Daddy Wabash and
Mama Catalina family is stable because the
parents have been together for a long time,
and they are both lifers who do not have bad
problems with drugs.

This family is only one of numerous
families active now. If there is any trend at
this prison, it is for the new inmates to be
part of established gangs with street
connections instead of being members of
prison families. From my point of view, that
makes prison a worse place to live. The
breakdown of the American family weakens
society no matter where it happens.

Professional Writer

Living In Two Worlds

Marcus Mabry

Coming from a poor family in New Jersey, Marcus Mabry encountered a very different part of society at Stanford University, a prestigious and expensive private school across the continent. Returning home made him all the more aware of the disparity between rich and poor, black and white. This essay was published in Newsweek on Campus.

1   A round, green cardboard sign hangs from a string proclaiming, "We built a proud new feeling," the slogan of a local supermarket. It is a souvenir from one of my brother's last jobs. In addition to being a bagger, he's worked at a fast-food restaurant, a gas station, a garage and a textile factory. Now, in the icy clutches of the Northeastern winter, he is unemployed. He will soon be a father. He is 19 years old.

2   In mid-December I was at Stanford, among the palm trees and weighty chore of academe. And all I wanted to do was get out. I joined the rest of the undergrads in a chorus of excitement, singing the praises of Christmas break. No classes, no midterms, no finals . . . and no freshmen! (I'm a resident assistant.) Awesome! I was looking forward to escaping. I never gave a thought to what I was escaping to.

3   Once I got home to New Jersey, reality returned. My dreaded freshmen had been replaced by unemployed relatives; badgering professors had been replaced by hard-working single mothers, and cold classrooms by dilapidated bedrooms and kitchens. The room in which the "proud new feeling" sign hung contained the belongings of myself, my mom and my brother. But for these two weeks it was mine. They slept downstairs on couches.

4   Most students who travel between the universes of poverty and affluence during breaks experience similar conditions, as well as the guilt, the helplessness and, sometimes, the embarrassment associated with them. Our friends are willing to listen, but most of them are unable to imagine the pain of the impoverished lives that we see every six months. Each time I return home I feel further away from the realities of poverty in America and more ashamed that they are allowed to persist. What frightens me most is not that the American socioeconomic system permits poverty to continue, but that by participating in that system I share some of the blame.

5   Last year I lived in an on-campus apartment, with a (relatively) modern bathroom, kitchen and two bedrooms. Using summer earnings, I added some expensive prints, a potted palm and some other plants, making the place look like the more-than-humble abode of a New York City Yuppie. I gave dinner parties, even a *soirée française*.

6   For my roommate, a doctor's son, this kind of life was nothing extraordinary. But my mom was struggling to provide a life

for herself and my brother. In addition to working 24-hour-a-day cases as a practical nurse, she was trying to ensure that my brother would graduate from high school and have a decent life. She knew that she had to compete for his attention with drugs and other potentially dangerous things that can look attractive to a young man when he sees no better future.

7   Living in my grandmother's house this Christmas break restored all the forgotten, and the never acknowledged, guilt. I had gone to boarding school on a full scholarship since the ninth grade, so being away from poverty was not new. But my own growing affluence has increased my distance. My friends say that I should not feel guilty: what could I do substantially for my family at this age, they ask. Even though I know that education is the right thing to do, I can't help but feel, sometimes, that I have it too good. There is no reason that I deserve security and warmth, while my brother has to cope with potential unemployment and prejudice. I, too, encounter prejudice, but it is softened by my status as a student in an affluent and intellectual community.

8   More than my sense of guilt, my sense of helplessness increases each time I return home. As my success leads me further away for longer periods of time, poverty becomes harder to conceptualize and feels that much more oppressive when I visit with it. The first night of break, I lay in our bedroom, on a couch that let out into a bed that took up the whole room, except for a space heater. It was a little hard to sleep because the springs from the couch stuck through at inconvenient spots. But it would have been impossible to sleep anyway because of the groans coming from my grandmother's room next door. Only in her early 60s, she suffers from many chronic diseases and couldn't help but moan, then pray aloud, then moan, they pray aloud.

9   This wrenching of my heart was interrupted by the 3 A.M. entry of a relative who had been allowed to stay at the house despite rowdy behavior and threats toward the family in the past. As he came into the house, he slammed the door, and his heavy steps shook the second floor as he stomped into my grandmother's room to take his place, at the foot of her bed. There he slept, without blankets on a bare mattress. This was the first night. Later in the vacation, a Christmas turkey and a Christmas ham were stolen from my aunt's refrigerator on Christmas Eve. We think the thief was a relative. My mom and I decided not to exchange gifts this year because it just didn't seem festive.

10   A few days after New Year's I returned to California. The Northeast was soon hit by a blizzard. They were there, and I was here. That was the way it had to be, for now. I haven't forgotten; the ache of knowing their suffering is always there. It has to be kept deep down, or I can't find the logic in studying and partying while people, my people, are being killed by poverty. Ironically, success drives me away from those I most want to help by getting an education.

11   Somewhere in the midst of all that misery, my family has built within me "a proud feeling." As I travel between the two worlds it becomes harder to remember just how proud I should be—not just because of where I have come from and where I am going, but because of where they are. The fact that they survive in the world in which they live is something to be very proud of, indeed. It inspires within me a sense of tenacity and accomplishment that I hope every college graduate will someday possess.

▌ EXERCISE 1

1. What is the thesis of Mabry's essay?

2. What is the purpose of this comparative study? Is Mabry only showing differences or is he making a point—for instance, about one standard of life having a higher quality?

3. What are the main points used for comparison?

4. Does poverty make people more considerate of others in the same condition?

5. How does Mabry draw strength from contemplating the misery of his family?

PRACTICING PATTERNS OF COMPARISON AND CONTRAST

▌ EXERCISE 2

Fill in the blanks to complete the comparisons and contrasts in the following point-by-point outlines.

Point-by-Point

John: Before and after marriage

  I. Way of talking (content and manner)

    A. _____

    B. John: After

  II. _____

    A. John: Before

    B. John: After

 III. _____

    A. John: Before

    B. _____

Subject-by-Subject

Two vans: Nissan Quest and Dodge Caravan (would be more specific if for a particular year)

  I. Quest

    A. Horsepower and gears

    B. _____

    C. Cargo area

  II. Caravan

    A. _____

    B. Safety

    C. _____

TOPICS FOR ESSAYS OF COMPARISON AND CONTRAST

Reading-Related Topics

1. "Families: Street and Prison": Monroe writes about "street families" as families with two heterosexual parents, but, of course, there are several kinds of families, including single parent, mother; single parent, father; extended family (with more than two generations together); single grandparent, grandmother; communal; and so on. Pick two kinds of families for your comparison and contrast essay.

2. "Living in Two Worlds": Write about a similar situation in which you or someone you know has had significant experiences in two contrasting environments. The two situations might be home and work, home and school, your home and the home of a friend, your home and the home of a relative, your home in this country and the home you had in another country. Consider using points such as physical surroundings, behavior of people, attitudes of others, and your attitude.

Career-Related Topics

3. Compare and contrast two products or services, with the purpose of showing that one is better.

4. Compare and contrast two management styles or two working styles.

5. Compare and contrast two career fields to show that one is better for you.

6. Compare and contrast a public school and a business.

7. Compare and contrast an athletic team and a business.

General Topics

The following topics refer to general subjects. Provide specific names and detailed information as you develop your ideas by using the 4 *P*'s.

8. Musical styles
9. Romantic attachments
10. Sitcoms
11. Businesses (selling the same product)

12. Methods of disciplining children
13. Love and infatuation
14. Courage and recklessness
15. Relatives
16. Jobs you have held
17. Passive student and active student
18. Weddings
19. Neighborhoods
20. Actors or other performers

WRITER'S GUIDELINES AT A GLANCE: COMPARISON AND CONTRAST

Work with the 4 *P*'s:

1. Purpose: Decide whether you want to inform (show relationships) or persuade (show that one side is better).
2. Points: Decide which ideas you will apply to each side.
3. Patterns: Decide whether to use subject-by-subject or point-by-point organization.
4. Presentation: Decide to what extent you should develop your ideas. Be sure to use cross-references to make connections and to use examples and details to support your views.
5. Your basic subject-by-subject outline will probably look like this:

    I. Subject 1
        A. Point 1
        B. Point 2
    II. Subject 2
        A. Point 1
        B. Point 2

6. Your basic point-by-point outline will probably look like this:

    I. Point 1
        A. Subject 1
        B. Subject 2
    II. Point 2
        A. Subject 1
        B. Subject 2

11

Definition: Clarifying Terms

WRITING ESSAYS OF DEFINITION

Most definitions are short; they consist of a synonym (a word that has the same meaning as the term to be defined), a phrase, or a sentence. For example, we might say that a hypocrite is a person "professing beliefs or virtues he or she does not possess." Terms can also be defined by *etymology,* or word history. *Hypocrite* once meant "actor" (*hypocrites*) in Greek because an actor was pretending to be someone else. We may find this information interesting and revealing, but the history of a word may be of no use because the meaning has changed drastically over the years. Sometimes definitions occupy a paragraph or an entire essay. The short definition is called a *simple definition;* the longer one is known as an *extended definition.*

Techniques for Development

Essays of definitions can take many forms. Among the more common techniques for writing a paragraph of definition are the patterns we have worked with in previous chapters. Consider each of those patterns when you need to write an extended definition. For a particular term, some forms will be more useful than others; use the pattern or patterns that best fulfill your purpose.

Each of the following questions takes a pattern of writing and directs it toward definition.

- Narration
  Can I tell an anecdote or story to define this subject (such as *jerk, humanitarian,* or *patriot*)? This form may overlap with description and exemplification.

- Description
  Can I describe this subject (such as *a whale* or *the moon*)?

- Exemplification
  Can I give examples of this subject (such as naming individuals, to provide examples of *actors, diplomats,* or *satirists*)?

- Analysis by Division
  Can I divide this subject into parts (for example, the parts of a *heart, cell,* or *carburetor*)?

- Process Analysis
  Can I define this subject (such as *lasagna, tornado, hurricane, blood pressure,* or any number of scientific processes) by describing how to make it or how it occurs? (Common to the methodology of communicating in science, this approach is sometimes called the "operational definition.")

- Cause and Effect
  Can I define this subject (such as *a flood, a drought, a riot,* or *a cancer*) by its causes and effects?

- Classification
  Can I group this subject (such as kinds of *families, cultures, religions,* or *governments*) into classes?

Subject	Class	Characteristics
A republic	is a form of government	in which power resides in the people (the electorate).

- Comparison and Contrast
  Can I define this subject (such as *extremist* or *patriot*) by explaining what it is similar to and different from? If you are defining *orangutan* to a person who has never heard of one but is familiar with the gorilla, then you could make comparison-and-contrast statements. If you want to define *patriot,* then you might want to stress what it is not (the contrast) before you explain what it is: a patriot is not a one-dimensional flag waver, not someone who hates "foreigners" because America is always right and always best.

When you use prewriting strategies to develop ideas for a definition, you can effectively consider all the patterns you have learned by using a modified clustering form. Put a double bubble around the subject to be defined. Then put a single bubble around the patterns and add appropriate words. If a pattern is not relevant to what you are defining, leave it blank. If you want to expand your range of information, you could add a bubble for a simple dictionary definition and another for an etymological definition.

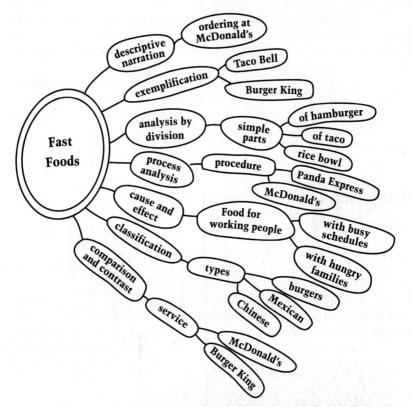

Bubble cluster showing how a term could be defined using different essay patterns.

Order

The organization of your extended definition is likely to be one of emphasis, but it may be space or time, depending on the subject material. You may use just one pattern of development for the overall sequence. If so, then you would employ the principles of organization discussed in previous chapters.

Introduction and Development

Consider these ways of introducing a definition: with a question, with a statement of what it is not, with a statement of what it originally meant, or with a discussion of why a clear definition is important. You may use a combination of these ways or all of them before you continue with your definition.

Development, whether in the form of sentences for the paragraph or of paragraphs for the essay, is likely to represent one or more of the patterns of narration, description, exposition (with its own subdivisions), and argumentation.

Whether you personalize a definition depends on your purpose and your audience. Your instructor may ask you to write about a word within the context of your experience or to write about it from a detached, clinical viewpoint.

EXAMINING ESSAYS OF DEFINITION

Student Writer

Modern Mother

Marie Maxwell

After having read numerous articles about women who are now free to pursue careers, Marie Maxwell reflected on her own situation. Her conclusion is that her situation is more typical than those she had read about. She wishes that were not true.

The modern mother, according to dozens of magazine articles, is a super being of incredible organization, patience, wisdom, and grooming. She is never cross with loved ones and never too tired for a game with her children. She wouldn't think of throwing a frozen dinner into the oven and calling it supper. She even has the courage (and the cleaning skills) to own a white carpet. She is a being apart, and I could never quite

Thesis measure up. <u>I believed that, until I recently decided there were far more women like me than there were Wonder Women.</u>

The ideal mother featured in the magazines has a lovely home, a handsome husband, and children who at all times appear to have just stepped from the pages of a clothing catalog. Her house is always clean and ready for drop-in guests, and should these guests arrive at supper time, so much

Contrast the better. My reality is a single-parent home. I have a son who I suspect is color-blind, judging from some of his outfits. Often when I return home from work, I must step carefully to avoid the assortment of

Examples books, clothes, and toys strewn from one room to the next. Unexpected company better not show up! As for feeding uninvited guests—they had better have an invitation if they expect to be fed.

Unlike me, the mothers in the articles always seem to have glamorous and exciting jobs. Most of them receive six-figure incomes and love their jobs (oops!) *careers*. They are

Examples fashion designers, doctors, or managers on their way up the corporate ladder. Every working day is another fascinating challenge to anticipate. I sigh wistfully as I read, and I think how dull my secretarial duties

Contrast are by comparison. I've received two promotions in eight years—hardly a mercurial

Effects   rise to the top. I generally enjoy my job; <u>it pays the bills and a little bit more</u>, and it <u>has enough variety</u> to prevent abysmal boredom. It's just that I feel somehow shamed by the way I earn my living after reading an article about the "new woman."

Most magazine writers choose as a subject a mother who has also returned to school, in addition to everything else she does. It depresses me to read that she has usually earned a 3.80 grade point average, seemingly effortlessly. Her family cheers her on and never seems to mind the time that school and homework demand from her. Even more disheartening is that her family members report with pride that she was able to make those grades without depriving them of their

Contrast   normal family life. <u>That certainly hasn't</u>
Example   <u>been my experience</u>. <u>Algebra</u>, for example, demanded so much of my time and energy that bitter words and sarcasm were routine in my household. When I was married, my husband was supportive only as long as my classes didn't disrupt his life.

Some modern mothers may indeed be just as they are described in the magazines, but I feel certain that there are many more just like me. My wish would be to have a writer

```
showcase a woman, if not with feet of clay,

at least shuffling her way artlessly through

a cluttered life and, at times, barely

coping. I might not admire her, but I

wouldn't feel inadequate, and I'm certain I

could identify with her. In fact, I think I

would like her.
```

PROFESSIONAL WRITER

Rambos of the Road

Martin Gottfried

Martin Gottfried is concerned about what happens to us—all of us—when we get behind the steering wheel of a car. We are transformed. What emerges is often something ugly and something mean. We become "Rambos of the Road."

1   The car pulled up and its driver glared at us with such sullen intensity, such hatred, that I was truly afraid for our lives. Except for the Mohawk haircut he didn't have, he looked like Robert DeNiro in "Taxi Driver," the sort of young man who, delirious for notoriety, might kill a president.

2   He was glaring because we had passed him and for that affront he pursued us to the next stoplight so as to express his indignation and affirm his masculinity. I was with two women and, believe it, was afraid for all three of us. It was nearly midnight and we were in a small, sleeping town with no other cars on the road.

3   When the light turned green, I raced ahead, knowing it was foolish and that I was not in a movie. He didn't merely follow, he chased, and with his headlights turned off. No matter what sudden turn I took, he followed. My passengers were silent. I knew they were alarmed, and I prayed that I wouldn't be called upon to protect them. In that cheerful frame of mind, I turned off my own lights so I couldn't be followed. It was lunacy. I was responding to a crazy *as* a crazy.

4   "I'll just drive to the police station," I finally said, and as if those were the magic words, he disappeared.

5   **Elbowing fenders**: It seems to me that there has recently been an epidemic of auto macho—a competition perceived and

expressed in driving. People fight it out over parking spaces. They bully into line at the gas pump. A toll booth becomes a signal for elbowing fenders. And beetle-eyed drivers hunch over their steering wheels, squeezing the rims, glowering, preparing the excuse of not having seen you as they muscle you off the road. Approaching a highway on an entrance ramp recently, I was strong-armed by a trailer truck so immense that its driver all but blew me away by blasting his horn. The behemoth was just inches from my hopelessly mismatched coupe when I fled for the safety of the shoulder.

6   And this is happening on city streets, too. A New York taxi driver told me that "intimidation is the name of the game. Drive as if you're deaf and blind. You don't hear the other guy's horn and you sure as hell don't see him."

7   The odd thing is that long before I was even able to drive, it seemed to me that people were at their finest and most civilized when in their cars. They seemed so orderly and considerate, so reasonable, staying in the right-hand lane unless passing, signaling all intentions. In those days you really eased into highway traffic, and the long, neat rows of cars seemed mobile testimony to the sanity of most people. Perhaps memory fails, perhaps there were always testy drivers, perhaps—but everyone didn't give you the finger.

8   A most amazing example of driver rage occurred recently at the Manhattan end of the Lincoln Tunnel. We were four cars abreast, stopped at a traffic light. And there was no moving even when the light had changed. A bus had stopped in the cross traffic, blocking our paths: it was a normal-for-New-York-City *gridlock*. Perhaps impatient, perhaps late for important appointments, three of us nonetheless accepted what, after all, we could not alter. One, however, would not. He would not be helpless. He would go where he was going even if he couldn't get there. A Wall Street type in suit and tie, he got out of his car and strode toward the bus, rapping smartly on its doors. When they opened, he exchanged words with the driver. The doors folded shut. He then stepped in front of the bus, took hold of one of its large windshield wipers and broke it.

9   The bus doors reopened and the driver appeared, apparently giving the fellow a good piece of his mind. If so, the lecture was wasted, for the man started his car and proceeded to drive directly *into the bus*. He rammed it. Even though the point at which he struck the bus, the folding doors, was its most *vulner-*

able point, ramming the side of a bus with your car has to rank very high on a futility index. My first thought was that it had to be a rented car.

10   **Lane merger**: To tell the truth, I could not believe my eyes. The bus driver opened his doors as much as they could be opened and he stepped directly onto the hood of the attacking car, jumping up and down with both his feet. He then retreated into the bus, closing the doors behind him. Obviously a man of action, the car driver backed up and rammed the bus again. How this exercise in absurdity would have been resolved none of us will ever know for at that point the traffic unclogged and the bus moved on. And the rest of us, we passives of the world, proceeded, our cars crossing a field of battle as if nothing untoward had happened.

11   It is tempting to blame such belligerent, uncivil and even neurotic behavior on the nuts of the world, but in our cars we all become a little crazy. How many of us speed up when a driver signals his intention of pulling in front of us? Are we resentful and anxious to pass him? How many of us try to squeeze in, or race along the shoulder at a lane merger? We may not jump on hoods, but driving the gantlet, we seethe, cursing not so silently in the safety of our steel bodies on wheels—fortresses for cowards.

12   What is within us that gives birth to such antisocial behavior and why, all of a sudden, have so many drivers gone around the bend? My friend Joel Katz, a Manhattan psychiatrist, calls it, "a Rambo pattern. People are running around thinking the American way is to take the law into your own hands when anyone does anything wrong. And what constitutes 'wrong'? Anything that cramps your style."

13   It seems to me that it is a new America we see on the road now. It has the mentality of a hoodlum and the backbone of a coward. The car is its weapon and hiding place, and it is still a symbol even in this. Road Rambos no longer bespeak a self-reliant, civil people tooling around in family cruisers. In fact, there aren't families in these machines that charge headlong with their brights on in broad daylight, demanding we get out of their way. Bullies are loners, and they have perverted our liberty of the open road into drivers' license. They represent an America that derides the values of decency and good manners, then . roam the highways riding shotgun and shrieking freedom. By allowing this to happen, the rest of us approve.

EXERCISE 1

1. A "Rambo of the Road" is a driver experiencing road rage. What is the meaning of the term *road rage*?

2. What is Joel Katz's definition of "a Rambo pattern"?

3. Who are responsible for the people who act out the Rambo pattern?

4. How many of the essay patterns—descriptive narration, exemplification, analysis by division, process analysis, cause and effect, classification, and comparison and contrast—does Gottfried use to write his extended definition? Indicate them below.

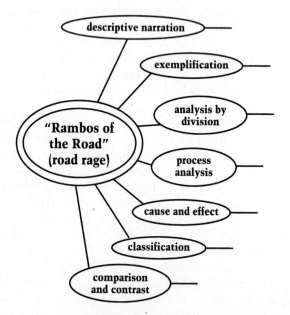

PRACTICING PATTERNS OF DEFINITION

EXERCISE 2

Fill in the double bubble with a term to be defined. You might want to define *culturally diverse society, educated person, leader, role model, friend, puppy love, true love, success,* or *intelligence.* Then fill in at least one more bubble on the right for each essay pattern. If the pattern does not apply (that is, if it would not provide useful information for your definition), mark it NA ("not applicable").

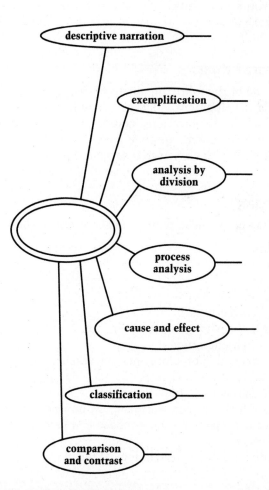

TOPICS FOR ESSAYS OF DEFINITION

Reading-Related Topics

1. "Modern Mother": Using Maxwell's essay as an example, define one of these terms (the one you select should apply to you or people you know): *modern mother, modern father, modern grandmother, modern grandfather, modern wife, modern husband, modern parents, modern kid(s).*

2. "Rambos of the Road": Define *road rage* as the term relates to Gottfried's essay. Of all the patterns of writing, exemplification and cause and effect will probably be the most useful. Personalize your essay by discussing your own feelings, the behavior of people you know, and the behavior of those you have observed on the roads.

Career-Related Topics

3. Define one of the following terms by using the appropriate pattern(s) of development (such as exemplification, cause and effect, descriptive narration, comparison and contrast): *total quality management, quality control, downsizing, outsourcing, business ethics, customer satisfaction, cost effectiveness.*

General Topics

Write an essay of extended definition about one of these terms.

4. Terrorism
5. Homelessness
6. Astrology
7. Depression
8. Political correctness
9. "Wannabe" (surfer, gangster, cool, tough guy, athlete, sexy, intellectual, parent, student)
10. A good coach, doctor, clergy person, teacher, police officer
11. The Good Life
12. Domestic violence
13. Addiction (perhaps concentrating on one substance or activity such as alcoholism, smoking tobacco, or gambling)
14. A good sport
15. Psychotic (or another psychological term)

WRITER'S GUIDELINES AT A GLANCE: DEFINITION

1. Use clustering to consider other patterns of development that may be used to define your term.

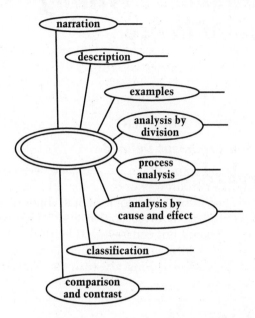

2. The organization of your extended definition is likely to be one of emphasis, but it may be space or time, depending on the subject material. You may use just one pattern of development for the overall organization.
3. Consider these ways of introducing a definition: with a question, with a statement of what it is not, with a statement of what it originally meant, or with a discussion of why a clear definition is important. You may use a combination of these ways before you continue with your definition.
4. Whether you personalize a definition depends on your purpose and your audience. Your instructor may ask you to write about a word within the context of your own experience or to write about it from a detached, clinical viewpoint.

12

Argument: Writing to Influence

WRITING ESSAYS OF ARGUMENT

Persuasion and Argument Defined

Persuasion is a broad term. When we persuade, we try to influence people to think in a certain way or to do something.

Argument is persuasion on a topic about which reasonable people disagree. Argument involves controversy. Whereas exercising appropriately is probably not controversial because reasonable people do not dispute the idea, an issue such as gun control is. In this chapter we will be concerned mainly with the kind of persuasion that involves argument.

Techniques for Developing Essays of Argument

Statements of argument are informal or formal in design. An opinion column in a newspaper is likely to have little set structure, whereas an argument in college writing is likely to be tightly organized. Nevertheless, the opinion column and the college paper have much in common. Both provide a proposition, which is the main point of the argument, and both provide support, which is the evidence or the reasons that back up the proposition.

For a well-structured college essay, an organization plan is desirable. Consider these elements when you write an essay of argument, and ask yourself the following questions as you develop your ideas:

> *Background:* What is the historical or social context for this controversial issue?
>
> *Proposition* (the thesis of the essay): What do I want my audience to believe or do?

156

Qualification of proposition: Can I limit my proposition so that those who disagree cannot easily challenge me with exceptions? If, for example, I am in favor of using animals for scientific experimentation, am I concerned only with medical experiments or with any use, including experiments for the cosmetic industry?

Refutation (taking the opposing view into account, mainly to point out its fundamental weakness): What is the view on the other side, and why is it flawed in reasoning and/or evidence?

Support: In addition to sound reasoning, can I use appropriate facts, examples, statistics, and opinions of authorities?

Components of Your Essay

The basic form for an essay of argument includes the proposition (the thesis of the essay), the refutation, and support, though the refutation is often omitted. The support sentences are, in effect, *because* statements; that is, the proposition is valid *because* of the support. Your organization should look something like this:

Proposition (thesis): It is time to pass a national law restricting smoking in public places.

I. Discomfort of the nonsmoker (support 1)
II. Health of the nonsmoker (support 2)
III. Cost to the nation (support 3)

Kinds of Evidence

In addition to sound reasoning generally, you can use these kinds of evidence.

First, you can offer facts. Martin Luther King, Jr., was killed in Memphis, Tennessee, on April 4, 1968. Because an event that has happened is true and can be verified, this statement about King is a fact. But that James Earl Ray acted alone in killing King is to some a questionable fact. That King was the greatest of all civil rights leaders is also opinion because it cannot be verified.

Some facts are readily accepted because they are general knowledge—you and your reader know them to be true, because they can be or have been verified. Other "facts" are based on personal observation and are reported in various publications but may be false or questionable. You should always be concerned about the reliability of the source for both the information you use and the information used by those with other viewpoints. Still other "facts" are genuinely debatable because of their complexity or the incompleteness of the knowledge available.

Second, you can cite examples. Keep in mind that you must present a sufficient number of examples and that the examples must be relevant.

Third, you can present statistics. Statistics are facts and data of a numerical kind that are classified and tabulated in order to present significant information about a given subject.

Avoid presenting a long list of figures; select statistics carefully and relate them to things familiar to your reader. The millions of dollars spent on a war in a single week, for example, become more comprehensible when expressed in terms of what the money would purchase in education, highways, or urban renewal.

To test the validity of statistics, either yours or your opponent's, ask: Who gathered them? Under what conditions? For what purpose? How are they used?

Fourth, you can cite evidence from, and opinions of, authorities. Most readers accept facts from recognized, reliable sources—governmental publications, standard reference works, and books and periodicals published by established firms. In addition, they will accept evidence and opinions from individuals who, because of their knowledge and experience, are recognized as experts.

In using authoritative sources as proof, keep these points in mind:

- Select authorities who are generally recognized as experts in their field.
- Use authorities who qualify in the field pertinent to your argument.
- Select authorities whose views are not biased.
- Try to use several authorities.
- Identify the authority's credentials clearly in your essay.

EXAMINING ESSAYS OF ARGUMENT

Student Writer

Someone is Listening

Michael Holguin

Student Michael Holguin grew up with shame and guilt because he believed he was wicked. His belief was implanted and reinforced by all institutions he encountered—family, church, school, government. It was wrong in every sense to be sexually attracted to people of the same gender. Therefore, he knew he must keep his mortal sin a secret.

Proposition

In today's society there is a form of child abuse that not even Oprah talks about. Unlike some other forms of abuse, it knows no limitations—no ethnic, no religious, no educational, and no socioeconomic boundaries. Lives are destroyed by parents who act in fear and ignorance. Dreams are shattered by the cruel and hurtful words of friends. Every day, hundreds of gay youths hide in their rooms and cry from pain caused by the mean and careless behavior of those who claim to love them.

Support 1: attacks at church

In a Judeo-Christian society it is common for families to attend church with their children. The pastor in many of these churches stands at the podium and announces, "Homosexuals are an abomination unto the Lord." The church walls shake from the resounding "Amen" from the congregation. The pastor continues, "Homosexuals are sick. Perverted. They are a danger to our children." In agreement the congregation once more says, "Amen." I know how this feels. As a gay person, I recall the pain of many such Sundays during my childhood. I prayed extra hard for God's cure before someone would find out my

secret and embarrass me and my family, because
I remembered what had happened to Jason the
year before. So I kept answering the altar
call every Sunday when the unwanted feeling
wouldn't go away. The fear of rejection and
eternal damnation made me too terrified to
confide in anyone or to ask for help. After
all, my parents seemed to tell me I deserved
such a fate every time they said, "Amen."

Support 2: attacks at school

Every day at school became more difficult
to endure. I faced the jokes in the locker
room. Even my best friend told some, and
sometimes, to keep from being discovered, I
told some. At this point, how much self-esteem
could I have had? I cringed when my coach urged
us to "kick those faggots' asses" but I still
kicked. Yet every day my feelings were denied.
My health teacher told us, "Someday you will
all grow up and get married and have children."
I couldn't understand why I had no such desire.
I would turn on the television, and there would
be a cop show on. This week's criminal was a
gay child molester . . . again. I think
"Baretta" had the same story the week before. I
changed the station to "Barney Miller," where
there was an old man wearing a polyester
jumpsuit and a silk scarf around his neck, and
talking with a lisp. Couldn't they drop the

lisp just once? I wonder. I cringe, thinking this is my inevitable fate, my curse.

Support 3: attacks at home

By the time I reached my teen years, I'd heard and seen so much negativity toward my "condition" that my life at home became plagued with constant fears. I became afraid of rejection. I knew my Christian family would think I was sick, perverted, and dangerous to children. Dad would be disappointed, even though I had six brothers to carry on the family name. Mom would not want me around because she'd worry about what to tell Grandma and Grandpa. My brother would pretend he didn't know me at school.

Support 4: attacks on friends

My fears were reinforced by close-up examples. Once I had a friend named Daniel, who was the son of a local preacher. I don't know where Daniel got the nerve at the age of twelve to tell his parents he was gay, but that's what he did. It was also at the age of twelve that his father put him out on the street after all the beatings failed to cure him. Daniel managed to stay alive on the streets as a prostitute. He's in prison now, dying of AIDS. The fear of rejection was real.

I learned how to fit in out of fear of humiliation but especially out of fear of physical abuse. I had seen Daniel's father and brothers beat him up almost daily. An even earlier memory from when I was very young involved a boy named Terry, who everyone knew was different. Some kids had figured Terry out. One day behind the school, way out in the field, four kids beat Terry up. Kicking and slugging him as he fell to the ground, they called out "Sissy" and "Queer" as they swung at him. We had only heard the word *queer* from the older boys, and no one was sure what it meant exactly. We hadn't encountered the word *faggot* yet. I suppose I didn't like Terry much either, but I felt bad as I watched in terror, knowing that the next time it could be me that they considered "different."

Support 5: pressure by society

<u>After years of living with low self-esteem, a battered self-image, and a secret life, one's psyche tends to give out.</u> The highest rate of teen suicide is among gay youths. In a recent five-year study, it was determined that fear of rejection was the number one cause of suicide among gay teenagers. After losing the loving environment of friends and families, many gays turn to other means of comfort. Drug and alcohol abuse is high among gays. Many turn to multiple lovers, looking for acceptance

and emotional support. The result of this has
been the devastating spread of AIDS. With
nowhere to go, suicide often seems to be the
only option. My friend Billy, when visiting
his younger sister at his mother's home,
would have to stay on the front porch and
talk through the screen door at his mother's
request. Last February, at the age of 19,
Billy drove up to the mountains and there
took his own life. Before he died he wrote on
the hood of his car, "God, help me." I recall
my own suicide attempt, which was the result
of my inability to deal with a life-style
everyone close to me was unable to accept. It
was only my self-acceptance that eventually
saved me from being a statistic.

**Reflection
on thesis**

When planning a family, people should ask
themselves, "Will I love my children for who
they are, or will I love them only if they're
what I want them to be?" If people answer the
latter, they shouldn't be parents. The same
kind of thing might be said for others who
are responsible for helping children develop.
Abuse comes in many forms, and ignorance and
self-centeredness are usually its foundation.
Parents, preachers, teachers, clergy,
friends—please be cautious of what you say.
The children are listening.

PROFESSIONAL WRITER

How About Low-Cost Drugs for Addicts?

Louis Nizer

According to Louis Nizer in this article, first published in the New York Times, *if we want to win the war against drugs, we should change the strategy and, instead, sell drugs to addicts.*

1   We are losing the war against drug addiction. Our strategy is wrong. I propose a different approach.

2   The Government should create clinics, manned by psychiatrists, that would provide drugs for nominal charges or even free to addicts under controlled regulations. It would cost the Government only 20 cents for a heroin shot, for which the addicts must now pay the mob more than $100, and there are similar price discrepancies in cocaine, crack and other such substances.

3   Such a service, which would also include the staff support of psychiatrists and doctors, would cost a fraction of what the nation now spends to maintain the land, sea and air apparatus necessary to interdict illegal imports of drugs. There would also be a savings of hundreds of millions of dollars from the elimination of the prosecutorial procedures that stifle our courts and overcrowd our prisons.

4   We see in our newspapers the triumphant announcements by Government agents that they have intercepted huge caches of cocaine, the street prices of which are in the tens of millions of dollars. Should we be gratified? Will this achievement reduce the number of addicts by one? All it will do is increase the cost to the addict of his illegal supply.

5   Many addicts who are caught committing a crime admit that they have mugged or stolen as many as six or seven times a day to accumulate the $100 needed for a fix. Since many of them need two or three fixes a day, particularly for crack, one can understand the terror in our streets and homes. It is estimated that there are in New York City alone 200,000 addicts, and this is typical of cities across the nation. Even if we were to assume that only a modest percentage of a city's addicts engage in criminal conduct to obtain the money for the habit, requiring multiple muggings and thefts each day, we could nevertheless account for many of the tens of thousands of crimes each day in New York City alone.

6   Not long ago, a Justice Department division issued a report stating that more than half the perpetrators of murder and other serious crimes were under the influence of drugs. This symbolizes the new domestic terror in our nation. This is why our citizens are unsafe in broad daylight on the most traveled thoroughfares. This is why typewriters and television sets are stolen from offices and homes and sold for a pittance. This is why parks are closed to the public and why murders are committed. This is why homes need multiple locks, and burglary systems, and why store windows, even in the most fashionable areas, require iron gates.

7   The benefits of the new strategy to control this terrorism would be immediate and profound.

8   First, the mob would lose the main source of its income. It could not compete against a free supply for which previously it exacted tribute estimated to be hundreds of millions of dollars, perhaps billions, from hopeless victims.

9   Second, pushers would be put out of business. There would be no purpose in creating addicts who would be driven by desperate compulsion to steal and kill for the money necessary to maintain their habit. Children would not be enticed. The mob's macabre public-relations program is to tempt children with free drugs in order to create customers for the future. The wave of street crimes in broad daylight would diminish to a trickle. Homes and stores would not have to be fortresses. Our recreational areas could again be used. Neighborhoods would not be scandalized by sordid street centers where addicts gather to obtain their supply from slimy merchants.

10   Third, police and other law-enforcement authorities, domestic or foreign, would be freed to deal with traditional non-drug crimes.

11   There are several objections that might be raised against such a salutary solution.

12   First, it could be argued that by providing free drugs to the addict we would consign him to permanent addiction. The answer is that medical and psychiatric help at the source would be more effective in controlling the addict's descent than the extremely limited remedies available to the victim today. I am not arguing that the new strategy will cure everything. But I do not see many addicts being freed from their bonds under the present system.

13   In addition, as between the addict's predicament and the safety of our innocent citizens, which deserves our primary concern? Drug-induced crime has become so common that almost every citizen knows someone in his immediate family or among his friends who has been mugged. It is these citizens who should be our chief concern.

14   Another possible objection is that addicts will cheat the system by obtaining more than the allowable free shot. Without discounting the resourcefulness of the bedeviled addict, it should be possible to have Government cards issued that would be punched so as to limit the free supply in accord with medical authorization.

15   Yet all objections become trivial when matched against the crisis itself. What we are witnessing is the demoralization of a great society: the ruination of its school children, athletes and executives, the corrosion of the workforce in general.

16   Many thoughtful sociologists consider the rapidly spreading drug use the greatest problem that our nation faces—greater and more real and urgent than nuclear bombs or economic reversal. In China, a similar crisis drove the authorities to apply capital punishment to those who trafficked in opium—an extreme solution that arose from the deepest reaches of frustration.

17   Free drugs will win the war against the domestic terrorism caused by illicit drugs. As a strategy, it is at once resourceful, sensible and simple. We are getting nowhere in our efforts to hold back the ocean of supply. The answer is to dry up demand.

EXERCISE 1

1. What is Nizer's proposition?

2. Which paragraphs (by number) contain the main support?

3. Which paragraphs (by number) contain the refutation?

4. What kinds of evidence (facts, examples, statistics, authoritative statement) does Nizer offer? Give specific examples.

PRACTICING PATTERNS OF ARGUMENT

EXERCISE 2

Fill in the blanks with supporting statements for each proposition. Each outline uses this pattern:

> Proposition
>
> I. Support
> II. Support
> III. Support

1. Proposition: Medically assisted suicide for the terminally ill should be illegal

   I. _____

   II. Better pain management offered

   III. Could be misused by unscrupulous doctors or patients' relatives

2. Proposition: Medically assisted suicide for the terminally ill should be legal

   I. _____

   II. The expense of care for the terminally ill

   III. The pain and suffering of the dying person

TOPICS FOR ESSAYS OF ARGUMENT

Reading-Related Topics

1. "Someone is Listening": Write an essay of argument in which you are the advocate for another type of "outsider" such as a minority in terms of race, religion, political or philosophical beliefs or medical condition.
2. "How About Low-Cost Drugs for Addicts?": Write an argument on the other side of this issue. The author provides some of the opposing views in his refutation toward the end of his essay.

Career-Related Topics

3. Write an essay of argument to convince people that workers at a particular company should or should not be laid off.
4. Write an essay of argument to convince people that workers in a particular service industry should or should not go on strike.

General Topics

The following are broad subject areas; you will have to limit your focus for an essay of argument. You may modify the topics to fit specific situations.

5. School dress code
6. School uniforms
7. Sex education
8. Sexual harassment
9. Juvenile justice
10. Endangered species legislation
11. Advertising tobacco
12. Homelessness
13. State-run lotteries
14. Jury reform
15. Legalizing prostitution
16. Censoring rap and/or rock music
17. Cost of illegal immigration
18. Installation of local traffic signs
19. Foot patrols by local police
20. Change in (your) college registration procedure
21. Local rapid transit
22. Surveillance by video (on campus, in neighborhoods, or in shopping areas)

23. Zone changes for stores selling liquor
24. Curfew for teenagers
25. Laws keeping known gang members out of parks

WRITER'S GUIDELINES AT A GLANCE: ARGUMENT

Ask yourself the following questions. Then consider which parts of the formal argument you should include in your essay.

1. *Background:* What is the historical or social context for this controversial issue?
2. *Proposition* (the thesis of the essay): What do I want my audience to believe or do?
3. *Qualification of proposition:* Can I limit my proposition so that those who disagree cannot easily challenge me with exceptions?
4. *Refutation* (taking the opposing view into account, mainly to point out its fundamental weakness): What is the view on the other side, and why is it flawed in reasoning and/or evidence?
5. *Support:* In addition to sound reasoning, can I use appropriate facts, examples, statistics, and opinions of authorities?

The basic pattern of an essay of argument is likely to be in this form:

Proposition (the thesis of the essay)

   I. Support 1
  II. Support 2
 III. Support 3

A

The Research Paper

THE LIBRARY

The main parts of the library pertaining to the research paper are the book collection and the periodical collection. Books are arranged on shelves by subject according to the Library of Congress system or the Dewey Decimal system. Periodicals, including newspapers, are stored in a variety of ways: in unbound form (very recent editions), in bound form, on microfilm, or on online computer systems.

Books

Today most academic and municipal libraries provide information about books on online computer terminals, with data banks accessible by author, title, subject, or other key words. Usually a printout of sources is available. Selecting key words and their synonyms is crucial to effective use of these online terminals. A combination of words will help you focus your search. In the following sample printout on the topic *animals and conservation*, the user has keyed in the topic and then clicked to the title to check for location and availability:

```
BOOK - Record 1 of 20 Entries Found                        Brief View
- - - - - - - - - - - - - - - - - - - - - - - - - - - - - - - - - - - - - - - -
Title:        The atlas of endangered species
Published:    New York : Macmillan : Toronto : Maxwell Macmillan Canada,
              1991.
Subjects:     Endangered species.
              Endangered plants.
              Nature conservation.
              Rare animals.
              Rare plants.
              Wildlife conservation.
              Environmental protection.
- - - - - - - - - - - - - - - - - - - - - - - - - - - - - - - + Page 1 of 2 - - - - - - - - - - -
Search Request: K=ANIMAL? AND CONSERVATION           MS<ENTER>=Book catalog
BOOK - Record 1 of 20 Entries Found                         Brief View
- - - - - - - - - - - - - - - - - - - - - - - - - - - - - - - - - - - - - - - -
Title:        The atlas of endangered species
- - - - - - - - - - - - - - - - - - - - - - - - - - - - - - - - - - - - - - - -
LOCATION:              CALL NUMBER              STATUS:
REFERENCE SHELVES      333.9516 At65             Not checked out
(Non-Circulating)
```

Printed Material Other Than Books

For the typical college research paper, the main printed nonbook sources are periodicals, such as newspapers, magazines, and journals. Various indexes will provide you with information for finding the source material you need. Depending on the library and the publication, periodicals are listed in indexes printed on paper or in electronic form. The most common index in bound volumes is the *Readers' Guide to Periodical Literature* (now also computerized). It indexes more than 200 popular magazines such as *Time* and *Newsweek*, which means that it is useful for basic research but not for more scholarly studies. The *New York Times* and numerous other metropolitan newspapers are also covered by indexes. For more academic searches, check with a reference librarian for indexes in specific fields such as anthropology or art. Indexes are usually kept in one area of the reference section. The following figure shows three sample entries from the *Readers' Guide:*

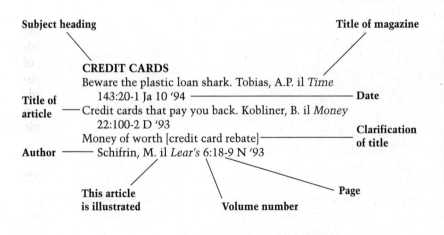

Subject heading

Title of magazine

CREDIT CARDS
Beware the plastic loan shark. Tobias, A.P. il *Time*
143:20-1 Ja 10 '94 —————————————— Date

Title of article — Credit cards that pay you back. Kobliner, B. il *Money*
22:100-2 D '93

Money of worth [credit card rebate] —————— Clarification of title

Author ——— Schifrin, M. il *Lear's* 6:18-9 N '93

This article is illustrated

Volume number

Page

Computerized Indexes and Other Online Services

Computerized indexes, such as *InfoTrac, Periodical Abstracts,* and *Newspaper Abstracts Ondisc,* can be accessed in basically the same way as the online book catalogs, using key words and word combinations. They provide source information, perhaps with printouts. Some indexes include short abstracts (brief summaries) of the individual entries. Some indexes even provide the full text of material.

One is *NEXIS*, an online service that can help you find sources and then provide the text of the original source material, all of which can be printed out.

You should be aware that an online essay originally published in, say, *Time* magazine, usually will be published without illustrations and in a different format. Therefore, it is important that you give full bibliographical information about your particular source (source citation instructions appear later in this chapter).

Government publications, pamphlets, and other materials are cataloged in several ways. Procedures for searching all electronic indexes and sources routinely are posted alongside terminals, and librarians are available for further explanations and demonstrations. Many libraries also have pamphlets listing the periodicals they carry, their arrangements with other libraries for sharing or borrowing materials, access to the Internet, databases stored on CD-ROMS, and various online services.

THE RESEARCH PAPER

The *research paper* is a long documented essay based on a thorough examination of your topic and supported by your explanations and by both references to and quotations from your sources. The traditional research paper in the style of the Modern Language Association, typically called MLA style, includes a title page (often omitted), a thesis and outline, a documented essay (text), and a list of sources (called "Works Cited," referring to the works used specifically in the essay).

This section will introduce you to eight steps for writing a research paper. Don't be apprehensive; if you can write an effective essay, you can write an effective research paper. Just pick a feasible topic and don't get behind schedule (the two main problems for students working on research papers). The form for documentation follows in the next section of this chapter.

Steps to Writing a Research Paper

Although specific aims and methods may vary from one research activity to another, most nonexperimental, objective research tasks depend on these basic steps. See the following explanation and then review the sample student work for illustration. Excerpts from a student final draft follow this discussion.

1. Select your topic, and make a scratch outline.

As soon as possible construct a thesis as you did for writing essays by choosing what you intend to write about (subject) and then by deciding how you will limit or focus your subject (treatment).

- Your topic should interest you and be appropriate in subject and scope for your assignment.
- Your topic should be researchable and covered in library and other relevant sources, such as the Internet. Avoid topics that are too subjective or are so new that good source material is not available.

In order to write a treatment for your subject, you may need to scan a general discussion of your topic area so you can consider it in perspective and begin to see the parts or aspects on which you will want to concentrate. Relevant sections of encyclopedias and comprehensive books, such as textbooks, are often useful in establishing the initial overview. At this point, the closer you can come to a well-defined topic with a functional scratch outline of its divisions, the more likely you are to make a smooth, rapid, effective journey through the process.

Student Example of Topic

Tentative thesis: Despite some valid criticism, the zoo as an

subject

institution will probably survive because of its roles in entertain-

treatment

ment, education, and conservation.

Student Example of Scratch Outline

I. Entertainment
   A. Money
   B. Problems
II. Conservation
   A. Science
   B. Breeding
III. Education
   A. General public
   B. Students
IV. Criticism
   A. Pro
   B. Con

V. Zoos of future
   A. Education
   B. Conservation

2. Find sources for your investigation.

With your topic and its divisions in mind, use the resources and the electronic databases available in your college library to identify books, articles, and other materials pertaining to your topic. The list of these items, called the *bibliography*, should be prepared on cards in the form appropriate for your assignment (MLA in this text). Seek different kinds of materials (books, periodicals, newspapers, electronic databases), different types of source information (primary, meaning coming from direct study, participation, observation, involvement; and secondary, meaning coming from indirect means—usually reporting on what others have done, observed, or been involved in), and credible writers (authorities and relatively unbiased, reliable reporters on your topic).

Student Examples

Periodical
   Diamond, Fared. "Playing God at the Zoo." *Discover* Mar. 1995: 79–85.
Book
   Douglas-Hamilton, Ian. *Battle for the Elephants*. New York: Viking, 1992.

3. Take notes.

Resist the temptation to write down everything that interests you. Instead, take notes that pertain to divisions of your topic as stated in your thesis or scratch outline. Locate, read, and take notes on the sources listed in the preliminary bibliography. Some of these sources need to be printed out from electronic databases, some photocopied, and some checked out. Your notes will usually be on cards, with each card indicating key pieces of information:

A. Division of topic (usually the Roman numeral part of your scratch outline or divisions of your thesis)
B. Identification of topic (by author's last name or title of piece)
C. Location of material (usually by page number)
D. Text of statement as originally worded (with quotation marks; editorial comments in brackets), summarized or paraphrased (in student's own words, without quotation marks), and statement of relevance of material, if possible

Student Example

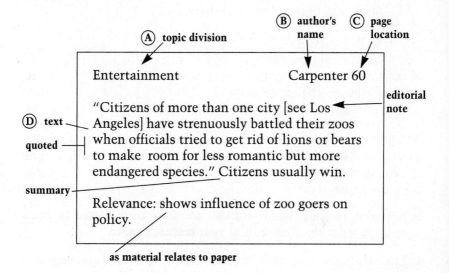

4. **Refine your thesis statement and outline to reflect more precisely what you intend to write.**

Student Example

Thesis: Throughout the world, despite determined opposition, the modern zoo with a new image and compound purpose is taking shape.

  I. Zoos as entertainment
     A. Attendance
     B. Income
     C. Customer preferences
 II. Captive breeding success
     A. National
        1. Bison
        2. California Condor
     B. International
        1. Arabian Oryx
        2. White Rhino
        3. Komodo dragon
III. Scientific success
     A. Embryo transfers

   B. Artificial insemination
   C. Test-tube fertilization
   D. Storage of eggs, sperm, and tissue
   E. Computer projects
      1. Lab studies
      2. Animal tracking
IV. Education
   A. Purpose—change attitude
   B. Basic idea—show animals in ecosystem
   C. School applications
 V. Different models of zoos
   A. Zoo/Park
   B. Safari zoo
   C. Regional zoo

5. **Referring to your thesis, outline, and note cards keyed to your outline, write the first draft of your research paper.**

6. **Evaluate your first draft, and amend it as needed (perhaps researching an area not well-covered for additional support material and adding or deleting sections of your outline to reflect the way your paper has grown).**

   Employ the writing process guidelines as you would in writing any other essay:

   - Write and then revise your assignment as many times as necessary for coherence, language, (usage, tone, and diction), unity, emphasis, support, and sentences (*CLUESS*).
   - Correct problems in fundamentals such as capitalization, omissions, punctuation, and spelling (*COPS*). Before writing the final draft, read your paper aloud to discover any errors or awkwardnesses of expression.

Use guidelines in this chapter (page 180) to include proper research paper form in documentation.

7. **Using the same form as on the preliminary bibliography, prepare a "Works Cited" section (a list of works you have referred to or quoted and identified by parenthetical markers in the text).**

8. **Submit your final research paper (and any preliminary material required by your instructor).**

The final draft will probably include these parts:

A. Title page (often omitted)
B. Outline (topical or sentence, as directed) and thesis
C. Documented text
D. List of sources used

Student Examples

- Title page

Zoos—An Endangered Species?

Michael Chung
Professor Lee Brandon
English 1A
5 May 1998

- Thesis and outline (previously given)
- Excerpt from the documented text (from pages 7–8)

In a spectacular captive breeding success in 1992, the National Zoo in Washington, D.C., may have saved the endangered Komodo dragon from extinction by successfully incubating thirty eggs. This ten-foot dangerous, ugly creature that resembles a

(statistics)
paraphrased
material

dinosaur numbers only somewhere around 5,000-8,000 in the wild but soon will be

citation

represented in numerous zoos (Browne C1). Now that the incubation process is established, the entire program offers opportunity to restock the Komodo's habitat in Indonesia.

Not all captive breeding projects can end with a reintroduction of the species to the wild. For those species, the zoos have turned

	to science, which has been used in a variety
here introduced with author's name and title	of ways. In "Preserving the Genetic Legacies," Karen F. Schmidt says:
long quotation—block-indented, no quotation marks needed	Zoos are increasingly adapting the latest in human and agricultural reproductive technologies to aid beleaguered species by boosting their numbers, increasing gene variety in small populations and
words omitted (ellipses)	controlling inbreeding. . . . Although still in the early stages, embryo transfers, artificial insemination and even test-tube fertilization are seen by zoologists as having real or potential
citation after period for long quotation	application in conserving endangered wildlife. (60)

These scientific endeavors began in the 1970s and now some of them are commonplace.

here introduced with author's name Female apes are on the pill and surrogate mother tigers are receiving embryos. Schmidt reports that the Cincinnati Zoo Center for

blended paraphrase and quotation Reproduction of Endangered Wildlife has frozen "eggs from a rare female Sumatran rhino that died, hoping one day to obtain some sperm and learn how to make test-tube

citation after quotation marks for short quotation rhino embryos" (60). In many zoos, eggs, sperm, and skin for DNA storage have been frozen in zoo labs, awaiting scientific development by future generations.

■ List of sources used

Works Cited (partial)

newspaper   Browne, Malcolm W. "They're Back! Komodos
Avoid Extinction." <u>N.Y. Times</u> 1 Mar. 1994:
C1, C4.

book   Douglas-Hamilton, Ian. <u>Battle for the
Elephants</u>. New York: Viking, 1992.

magazine   "Not Endangered." <u>The Economist</u> 13 Apr. 1991:
55-56.

web site   "Project Technology." <u>The Malaysian Elephant
Satelite Tracking Project</u>. <http://www.
si.edu/elephant/eleintro.htn.27 Apr. 1997>.

Internet   Rainey, James. "Dogfight at the Zoo." <u>Los
Angeles Times</u> 30 Jan. 1994: C1, C4.
<http://www.latimes.com/cgi-bin 1994. 29
Apr. 1997>.

magazine   Schmidt, Karen F. "Preserving the Genetic
Legacies." <u>U.S. News & World Report</u> 24 Aug.
1992: 60.

magazine   Tarpy, Cliff. "New Zoos." <u>National Geographic</u>
July 1993: 6-37.

magazine   Tudge, Colin. "Captive Audiences for Future
Conservation." <u>New Scientist</u> 28 Jan. 1995:
51.

**second piece
by same
author—book**   —— <u>Last Animals at the Zoo: How Mass Extinction Can Be Stopped</u>. London: Hutchinson Ra-
dius, 1991.

BIBLIOGRAPHY AND WORKS CITED, MLA STYLE

You will list source material in two phases of your research paper project: the preliminary bibliography and the works cited.

When you begin your research, make a list of works that may provide useful information on your topic. At this time, do not stop to make a careful examination and evaluation of each entry, although you should keep in mind that your material usually should come from a variety of sources and that they ideally should be objective, authoritative, and current. For various reasons, some items may not find their way into your research paper at all. As you read them, you may discover that some are superficial, poorly researched, overly technical, off the topic, or unavailable. The preliminary bibliography is nothing more than a list of sources to consider and select from.

The sources that are actually used in the paper—meaning those referred to by name or quoted—become part of the Works Cited list at the end of the final draft.

The MLA research paper form is commonly used for both the preliminary bibliography and the list of works cited. This format is unlike the formats used in catalogs and indexes. The following examples show the difference between printout forms from library files and the MLA research paper forms.

In using Internet material, consider that some of the material is a copy of well-edited, carefully selected text and that some is published by those who happen to have a server, a bit of computer expertise, and a desire to publish. Some of those writers and others may be biased, illogical, and foolish. As you research and develop your topic, you should evaluate all content, with special concern for anonymous Internet material. Note the difference between printout forms from library files and the MLA research paper forms.

Books

Printout Form

```
Author:       DiSilvestro, Roger L.
Title:        The African elephant: twilight in Eden
Published:    New York: Wiley, ©1991.
```

MLA Research Paper Form

DiSilvestro, Roger L. *The African Elephant: Twilight in Eden.* New York: Wiley, 1991.

Periodicals

Printout Form

```
AUTHOR:        Ormrod, Stefan A.
TITLE:         Boo for zoos.
SOURCE:        New Scientist v. 145 (Mar. 18 '95) p. 48
```

MLA Research Paper Form

Ormrod, Stefan A. "Boo for Zoos." *New Scientist* 18 Mar. 1995: 48.

Form for Printed Sources

Books

A Book by One Author
Adeler, Thomas L. *In a New York Minute.* New York: Harper, 1990.

An Anthology
List the name of the editor, followed by a comma, a space, and "ed."
Gunn, Giles, ed. *New World Metaphysics.* New York: Oxford UP, 1981.

Two or More Books by the Same Author
Walker, Alice. *The Color Purple: A Novel.* New York: Harcourt, 1982.
——— *Meridian.* New York: Harcourt, 1976.

A Book by Two or More Authors
Berry, Mary Frances, and John W. Blassingame. *Long Memory: The Black Experience in America.* New York: Oxford UP, 1981.
Danziger, James N., et al. *Computers and Politics: High Technology in American Local Governments.* New York: Columbia UP, 1982. (et al. for four or more)

A Book with a Corporate Author
Detroit Commission on the Renaissance. *Toward the Future.* Detroit: Wolverine, 1989.

Articles

Article in a Journal
Butterick, George. "Charles Olson's 'The Kingfishers' and the Poetics of Change." *American Poetry* 6.2 (1989): 28–59.

Article in a Weekly or Biweekly Magazine, Author Unknown
  "How to Stop Crib Deaths." *Newsweek* 6 Aug. 1973: 79.

Article in a Monthly or Bimonthly Magazine
  Browne, Malcolm W. "Locking Out the Hackers: There Are Ways
  to Keep Trespassers Out of Computer Systems." *Discover* Nov.
  1983: 30–40.

Newspaper Article
  Gregory, Tina. "When All Else Fails." *Philadelphia Inquirer* 2
  Apr. 1990: C12.

Editorial
  "The President's Failure." Editorial. *Charlotte* [N.C.] *Observer*
  20 Nov. 1987: 14A.

A Work in an Anthology

Booth, Wayne C. "The Scholar in Society." *Introduction to
  Scholarship in Modern Languages and Literatures.* Ed. Joseph
  Gibaldi. New York: MLA, 1981. 116–143.

An Article in an Encyclopedia

Schmitt, Barton D., and C. Henry Kempe. "Child Abuse." *The
  Encyclopedia Americana.* International ed. 1980.

Government Publications

United States. Dept. of Transportation. National Highway Traffic
  Safety Admin. *Driver Licensing Laws Annotated 1980.* Washington: GPO, 1980.

Citations from the *Congressional Record* require only a date and
page number.
  Congressional Record. 11 Sept. 1992: 12019–24.

Published Proceedings of a Conference

*Proceedings of the 34th Annual International Technical Com-
  munication Conference.* Denver, 10–13 May 1987. San Diego:
  Univelt, 1987.

Treat particular presentations in the proceedings as you would
pieces in a collection.

Wise, Mary R. "The Main Event Is Desktop Publishing." *Proceedings of the 34th International Technical Communication*

Conference. Denver, 10–13 May 1987. San Diego: Univelt, 1987.

A Lecture, Speech, or Address

Kosinski, Jerzy. Address. Opening General Session. NCTE Convention. Louisville, KY, 26 Mar. 1987.

A Personal Interview

Thomas, Carolyn. Personal interview. 5 Jan. 1998.

Dealing with Questions of Form for Electronic Sources

Formats vary widely in electronic media because of the rapidly changing systems, sources, and terms. As a general rule, provide information that indicates to your reader how he or she can find the material or, if it is no longer available, how you found it.

Form for World Wide Web Sources

These guidelines on MLA documentation style are the only ones available on the Internet that are authorized by the Modern Language Association of America.

Sources on the World Wide Web that students and scholars use in their research include scholarly projects, reference databases, the texts of books, articles in periodicals, and professional and personal sites. Entries in a works-cited list for such sources contain as many items from the list below as are relevant and available. Following this list are sample entries for some common kinds of Web sources. (For an authoritative explanation of the full MLA system of documentation, see the *MLA Handbook for Writers of Research Papers.*)

1. Name of the author, editor, compiler, or translator of the source (if available and relevant), reversed for alphabetizing and followed by an abbreviation, such as *ed.*, if appropriate
2. Title of a poem, short story, article, or similar short work within a scholarly project, database, or periodical (in quotation marks); or title of a posting to a discussion list or forum (taken from the subject line and put in quotation marks), followed by the description *Online posting*
3. Title of a book (underlined)
4. Name of the editor, compiler, or translator of the text (if relevant and if not cited earlier), preceded by the appropriate abbreviation, such as *Ed.*

5. Publication information for any print version of the source
6. Title of the scholarly project, database, periodical, or professional or personal site (underlined); or, for a professional or personal site with no title, a description such as *Home page*
7. Name of the editor of the scholarly project or database (if available)
8. Version number of the source (if not part of the title) or, for a journal, the volume number, issue number, or other identifying number
9. Date of electronic publication, of the latest update, or of posting
10. For a posting to a discussion list or forum, the name of the list or forum
11. The number range or total number of pages, paragraphs, or other sections, if they are numbered
12. Name of any institution or organization sponsoring or associated with the Web site
13. Date when the researcher accessed the source
14. Electronic address, or URL, of the source (in angle brackets)

Scholarly Project

Victorian Women Writers Project. Ed. Perry Willett. Apr.
   1997. Indiana U. 26 Apr. 1997 <http://www.indiana.
   edu/~letrs/vwwp/>.

Professional Site

Portuguese Language Page. U of Chicago. 1 May 1997
   <http://humanities.uchicago.edu/romance/port/>.

Personal Site

Lancashire, Ian. Home page. 1 May 1997 <http://www.
   chass.utoronto.ca:8080/~ian/index.html>.

Book

Nesbit, E[dith]. Ballads and Lyrics of Socialism. Lon-
   don, 1908. Victorian Women Writers Project. Ed. Perry
   Willett. Apr. 1997. Indiana U. 26 Apr. 1997 <http://
   www.indiana.edu/~letrs/vwwp/nesbit/ballsoc.html>.
Brewer, F. Cobham. The Dictionary of Phrase and Fable.
   London, 1894. Hypertext edition. Bibliomania: Data

Text Publishing Ltd. 1996. 9 Oct. 1997 <http://www.
bibliomania.com/Reference/PhraseAndFable/>.

Poem

Nesbit, E[dith]. "Marching Song." Ballads and Lyrics of
Socialism. London, 1908. Victorian Women Writers Project. Ed. Perry Willett. Apr. 1997. Indiana U. 26
Apr. 1997 <http://www.indiana.edu/~letrs/vwwp/nesbit/
ballsoc.html#p9>.

Article in a Reference Database

"Fresco." Britannica Online. Vers. 97.1.1. Mar. 1997.
Encyclopaedia Britannica. 29 Mar. 1997 <http://www.eb.
com:180>.

Atwood, Margaret. "Memento Mori—but First, Carpe Diem."
Rev. of Toward the End of Time, by John Updike. New
York Times Book Review 12 Oct. 1997: 9-10. The New
York Times Books on the Web. 1997. The New York Times
Company. 13 Oct. 1997 <http://search.nytimes.com/
books/97/10/12/reviews/971012.12atwoodt.html>.

Article in a Journal

Flannagan, Roy. "Reflection on Milton and Ariosto."
Early Modern Literary Studies 2.3 (1996):16 pars. 22
Feb. 1997 <http://unixg.ubc.ca:7001/0/e-sources/emls/
02-3/flanmilt.html>.

Article in a Magazine

Landsburg, Steven E. "Who Shall Inherit the Earth?"
Slate 1 May 1997. 2 May 1997 <http://www.slate.com/
Economics/97-05-01/Economics.asp>.

Keillor, Garrison. "Why Did They Ever Ban a Book This
Bad?" Salon 13 Oct. 1997. 14 Oct. 1997 <http://www.
salon1999.com/feature/>.

Posting to a Discussion List

Merrian, Joanne. "Spinoff: Monsterpiece Theatre." Online
posting. 30 Apr. 1994. Shaksper: The Global Electronic
Shakespeare Conference. 27 Aug. 1997 <http://www.arts.
ubc.ca/english/iemle/shak/MONSTERP_SPINOFF.txt>.

In parenthetical references in the text, works on the World Wide Web are cited just like printed works. For any type of source, you must include information in your text that directs readers to the correct entry in the works-cited list (see the *MLA Handbook*, sec. 5.2). Web documents generally do not have fixed page numbers or any kind of section numbering. If your source lacks numbering, you have to omit numbers from your parenthetical references. If your source includes fixed page numbers or section numbering (such as numbering of paragraphs), cite the relevant numbers. Give the appropriate abbreviation before the numbers: "(Moulthrop, pars. 19–20)." (*Pars.* is the abbreviation for *paragraphs.* Common abbreviations are listed in the *MLA Handbook*, sec. 6.4.) For a document on the Web, the page numbers of a printout should normally not be cited, because the pagination may vary in different printouts.

Other Electronic Sources
Online Computer Service
> Fineman, Howard. "A Brawl on Tobacco Road: How Bill Clinton—and the Democrats' 'Butt Man'—Is Maneuvering to Turn Joe Camel into Bob Dole's Willie Horton." <u>Newsweek</u> 15 July 1996: n. pag. Online. American Online. 11 July 1996.

CD-ROM
> Picasso: The Man, His Works, the Legend. CD-ROM. Danbury: Grolier Interactive, 1996.

DOCUMENTATION: PARENTHETICAL REFERENCES, MLA STYLE

Although you need not acknowledge a source for generally known information such as the dates of the Civil War or the names of the ships that carried Columbus and his followers to the New World, you must identify the exact source and location of each statement, fact, or original idea you borrow from another person or work.

In the text of the research paper, MLA requires only a brief parenthetical source reference keyed to a complete bibliographical entry in the list of works cited at the end of the essay. For most parenthetical references, you will need to cite only the author's last name and the number of the page from which the statement or idea was taken, and, if you mention the author's name in the text, the page number alone is sufficient. This format also allows you to include within the parentheses additional information, such as title or volume number, if it is needed for clarity. Documentation for some of the most common types of sources is discussed in the following sections.

References to Articles and Single-Volume Books

Articles and single-volume books are the two types of works you will be referring to most often in your research paper. When citing them, either mention the author's name in the text and note the appropriate page number in parentheses immediately after the citation or acknowledge both name and page number in the parenthetical reference, leaving a space between the two. If punctuation is needed, insert the mark outside the final parenthesis.

- Author's Name Cited in Text

   Marya Mannes has defined euthanasia as "the chosen alternative to the prolongation of a steadily waning mind and spirit by machines that will withhold death or to an existence that mocks life" (61).

- Author's Name Cited in Parentheses

   Euthanasia has been defined as "the chosen alternative to the prolongation of a steadily waning mind and spirit by machines that will withhold death or to an existence that mocks life" (Mannes 61).

- Corresponding Bibliographic Entry

   Mannes, Marya. *Last Rights.* New York: Morrow, 1973.

References to Works in an Anthology

When referring to a work in an anthology, either cite in the text the author's name and indicate in parentheses the page number in the anthology where the source is located, or acknowledge both name and page reference parenthetically.

- Author's Name Cited in Text

   One of the most widely recognized facts about James Joyce, in Lionel Trilling's view, "is his ambivalence toward Ireland, of

which the hatred was as relentless as the love was unfailing"
(153).

- Author's Name Cited in Parentheses

    One of the most widely recognized facts about James Joyce "is
    his ambivalence toward Ireland, of which the hatred was as re-
    lentless as the love was unfailing" (Trilling 153).

- Corresponding Bibliographic Entry

    Trilling, Lionel, "James Joyce in His Letters." *Joyce: A Col-
    lection of Critical Essays.* Ed. William M. Chace. Engle-
    wood Cliffs: Prentice-Hall, 1974.

References to Works of Unknown Authorship

If you borrow information or ideas from an article or book for
which you cannot determine the name of the author, cite the title
instead, either in the text of the paper or in parentheses, and include the page reference as well.

- Title Cited in the Text

    According to an article entitled "Going Back to Booze," surveys
    have shown that most adult alcoholics began drinking heavily
    as teenagers (42).

- Title Cited in Parentheses

    Surveys have shown that most adult alcoholics began drinking
    heavily as teenagers ("Going Back to Booze" 42).

- Corresponding Bibliographic Entry

    "Going Back to Booze." *Time* 31 Nov. 1979: 41–46.

References to Internet Material

Treat them as you would other material. If the author's name is not
available, give the title. Use page and paragraph numbers if they are
available.

References in Block Quotations

Quotations longer than four typewritten lines are indented ten
spaces without quotation marks, and their references are put outside end punctuation.

Implicit in the concept of Strange Loops is the concept of infinity, since what else is a loop but a way of representing an endless process in a finite way? And infinity plays a large role in many of Escher's drawings. Copies of one single theme often fit into each other, forming visual analogues to the canons of Bach. (Hofstadter 15)

- Corresponding Bibliographic Entry
  > Hofstadter, Douglas. *Gödel, Escher, Bach: An Eternal Golden Braid.* New York: Vintage, 1980.

PLAGIARISM

Careful attention to the rules of documentation will help you avoid *plagiarism*: the unacknowledged use of someone else's words or ideas. It occurs when a writer omits quotation marks when citing the exact language of a source, fails to revise completely a paraphrased source, or gives no documentation for a quotation or paraphrase. The best way to avoid this problem is to be attentive to the following details.

When you copy a quotation directly into your notes, check to be sure that you have put quotation marks around it. If you forget to include them when you copy, you might omit them in the paper as well.

When you paraphrase, keep in mind that it is not sufficient to change just a few words or rearrange sentence structure. You must completely rewrite the passage. One of the best ways to accomplish this is to read the material you want to paraphrase; then cover the page so that you cannot see it and write down the information as you remember it. Then, compare your version with the original and make any necessary changes in the note. If you cannot successfully rewrite the passage, quote it instead.

The difference between legitimate and unacceptable paraphrases can be seen in the following examples:

- Source

  > "What is unmistakably convincing and makes Miller's theatre writing hold is its authenticity in respect to the minutiae of American life. He is a first-rate reporter; he makes the details of his observation palpable." —Harold Clurman's introduction to *The Portable Arthur Miller*

- Unacceptable paraphrase

  What is truly convincing and makes Arthur Miller's theatrical writing effective is its authenticity. He is an excellent reporter and makes his observation palpable.

- Legitimate paraphrase

  The strength of Arthur Miller's dramatic art lies in its faithfulness to the details of the American scene and in its power to bring to life the reality of ordinary experience.

The differences between these two versions of Clurman's statement are enormous. The first writer has made some token changes, substituting a few synonyms (*truly* for *unmistakably*, *excellent* for *first-rate*), deleting part of the first sentence, and combining the two parts of the second sentence into a single clause. Otherwise, this is a word-for-word copy of the original, and if the note were copied into the paper in this form, the writer would be guilty of plagiarism. The second writer, on the other hand, has changed the vocabulary of the original passage and completely restructured the sentence so that the only similarity between the note and the source is the ideas.

Check to see that each of your research notes has the correct name and page number so that when you use information from that note in your paper, you will be able to credit it to the right source.

Writer's Guidelines at a Glance: The Research Paper

1. The research paper is a long documented essay based on a thorough examination of a topic and supported by explanations and by both references to and quotations from sources.
2. The research paper is no more difficult than other writing assignments if you select a good topic, use a systematic approach, and do not get behind with your work.
3. A systematic approach involves selecting a topic, developing a preliminary bibliography, taking notes keyed to divisions of your topic, creating a detailed outline based on your notes and insights, writing a rough draft with ideas supported by source material, revising the draft as many times as necessary, editing the

paper, making a list of the works cited, and writing the final draft.

4. Your library almost certainly mixes traditional and electronic indexes and sources; you should become familiar with them.

5. The MLA forms for works cited are different from those in indexes.

6. You can avoid plagiarism by giving credit when you borrow someone else's words or ideas.

HANDBOOK

This handbook presents rules and examples for grammar, usage, punctuation, and capitalization. One good way to practice basic writing skills is to write your own examples. In working with verb tense, for example, you could write sentences (perhaps similar to the model sentences) in which you apply the appropriate patterns. In working with punctuation, you could write sentences that demonstrate your ability to use different punctuation marks correctly.

SUBJECTS AND VERBS

The **subject** is what the sentence is about, and the **verb** indicates what the subject is doing or is being.

Subjects

You can recognize the **simple subject** by asking Who? or What? causes the action or expresses the state of being found in the verb.

1. The **simple subject** and the **simple verb** can be single or compound.

   My *friend* and *I* have much in common.

   My friend *came* and *left* a present.

2. Although the subject usually appears before the verb, it may follow the verb.

   From tiny acorns grow mighty *oaks.*

3. The command, or **imperative,** sentence has a "you" as the implied subject, and no stated subject.

   (*You* understood) Read the notes.

4. Be careful not to confuse a subject with an **object of a preposition.**

   The *foreman* (subject) of the *jury* (object of preposition) directs discussion.

192

Verbs

Verbs show action or express being in relation to the subject.

1. **Action verbs** suggest movement or accomplishment in idea or deed.

> He *dropped* the book. (movement)
>
> He *read* the book. (accomplishment)

2. **Being verbs** indicate existence.

> They *were* concerned.

3. Verbs may appear as single words or as phrases.

> He *led* the charge. (single word)
>
> She *is leading* the charge. (phrase)

4. Verbs that are joined by a coordinating conjunction such as *and* and *or* are called **compound verbs.**

> She *worked* for twenty-five years and *retired*.

5. Do not confuse verbs with **verbals;** verbals are verblike words that function as other parts of speech.

> The bird *singing* (participle acting as an adjective) in the tree is defending its territory.
>
> *Singing* (gerund acting as a noun subject) is fun.
>
> I want *to eat*. (infinitive acting as a noun object)

6. Do not confuse **adverbs** such as *never, not,* and *hardly* with verbs; they only modify verbs.

7. Do not overlook a part of the verb that is separated from another in a question.

> "Where *had* the defendant *gone* on that fateful night?"

KINDS OF SENTENCES

On the basis of number and kinds of clauses, sentences may be classified as simple, compound, complex, and compound-complex.

Clauses

1. A **clause** is a group of words with a subject and a verb that functions as a part or all of a complete sentence. There are two kinds of clauses: (1) independent (main) and (2) dependent (subordinate).

2. **An independent (main) clause is a group of words with a subject and verb that can stand alone and make sense.** An independent

clause expresses a complete thought by itself and can be written as a separate sentence.

> *I have the money.*

3. **A dependent clause, on the other hand, is a group of words with a subject and verb that depends on a main clause to give it meaning.** The dependent clause functions in the common sentence patterns as a noun, adjective, or adverb.

> *When I have the money*

Types of Sentences

Type	Definition	Example
Simple	One independent clause	She did the work well.
Compound	Two or more independent clauses	She did the work well, and she was paid well.
Complex	One independent clause and one or more dependent clauses	*Because she did the work well,* she was paid well.
Compound-Complex	Two or more independent clauses and one or more dependent clauses	*Because she did the work well,* she was paid well, and she was satisfied.

Punctuation

1. Use a comma before a coordinating conjunction (*for, and, nor, but, or, yet, so*) between two independent clauses.

> The movie was good, but the tickets were expensive.

2. Use a comma after a dependent clause (beginning with a subordinating conjunction such as *because, although, when, since,* or *before*) that occurs before the main clause.

> When the bus arrived, we quickly boarded.

3. Use a semicolon between two independent clauses in one sentence if there is no coordinating conjunction.

> The bus arrived; we quickly boarded.

4. Use a semicolon before and usually a comma after a conjunctive adverb (such as *however, otherwise, therefore, on the other*

hand, in fact), between two independent clauses (no comma after *then, also, now, thus,* and *soon*).

> The Dodgers have not played well this year; however, the Giants have won ten games in a row.

SENTENCE PROBLEMS

Fragments

1. A correct sentence signals completeness; a **fragment** signals incompleteness—it doesn't make sense. You would expect the speaker or writer of a fragment to say or write more or to rephrase it.

2. A **dependent clause** cannot stand by itself because it begins with a subordinating word.

> *Because* he left.
>
> *When* she worked.
>
> *Although* they slept.

3. A **verbal phrase,** a **prepositional phrase,** and an **appositive phrase** may carry ideas, but each is incomplete because it lacks a subject and verb.

> verbal phrase: *having studied hard all evening*
> sentence: Having studied hard all evening, John decided to retire.
>
> prepositional phrase: *in the store*
> sentence: She worked in the store.
>
> appositive phrase: *a successful business*
> sentence: Marks Brothers, a successful business, sells clothing.

4. Each complete sentence must have an **independent clause,** meaning a word or a group of words that contains a subject and a verb that can stand alone.

> *He enrolled* for the fall semester.

Comma Splices and Run-Ons

1. The **comma splice** consists of two independent clauses with only a comma between them.

> The weather was disappointing, we canceled the picnic. (A comma by itself cannot join two independent clauses.)

2. The **run-on** differs from the comma splice in only one respect: it has no comma between the independent clauses. Therefore, the run-on is two independent clauses with *nothing* between them.

> The weather was disappointing we canceled the picnic. (Independent clauses must be properly connected.)

Correcting Comma Splices and Run-Ons

1. Use a comma and a **coordinating conjunction** (*for, and, nor, but, or, yet, so*) to correct a comma splice or run-on.

> We cancelled the picnic, *for* the weather was disappointing.

2. Use a **subordinating conjunction** (such as *because, after, that, when, although, since, how, until, unless, before*) to make one clause dependent to correct a comma splice or run-on.

> *Because* the weather was disappointing, we canceled the picnic.

3. Use a **semicolon** (with or without a conjunctive adverb such as *however, otherwise, therefore, similarly, hence, on the other hand, then, consequently, also, thus*) to correct a comma splice or run-on.

> The weather was disappointing; we canceled the picnic.
>
> The weather was disappointing; *therefore*, we canceled the picnic.

4. Make each clause a separate sentence. For a comma splice, replace the comma with a period, and begin the second sentence (clause) with a capital letter. For a run-on, insert a period between the two independent clauses and begin the second sentence with a capital letter.

> The weather was disappointing. We canceled the picnic.

SENTENCE COMBINING

Coordination

If you intend to communicate two equally important and closely related ideas, you certainly will want to place them close together, probably in a **compound sentence** (two or more independent clauses).

1. When you combine two sentences by using a **coordinating conjunction,** drop the period, change the capital letter to a small letter, and insert a comma before the coordinating conjunction.

> I like your home, but I can visit for only three months.

2. When you combine two sentences by using a **semicolon,** replace the period with a semicolon and change the capital letter to a small letter. If you wish to use a conjunctive adverb, insert it after the semicolon and usually put a comma after it.

> I like your home. I can visit for only three months.
>
> I like your home; I can visit for only three months.
>
> I like your home; however, I can visit for only three months.

Subordination

If you have two ideas that are closely related, but one is secondary or dependent on the other, you may want to use a **complex sentence.**

> My neighbors are considerate. They never play loud music.
>
> Because my neighbors are considerate, they never play loud music.

1. If the dependent clause comes before the main clause, set it off with a comma.

> Before you dive, be sure there is water in the pool.

2. If the dependent clause comes after the main clause, set it off with a comma only if you use the word *though* or *although,* or if the words are not necessary to convey the basic meaning in the sentence.

> Be sure there is water in the pool before you dive.

Coordination and Subordination

At times you may want to show the relationship of three or more ideas within one sentence. If that relationship involves two or more main ideas and one or more supporting ideas, the combination can be stated in a **compound-complex sentence** (two or more independent clauses and one or more dependent clauses).

> Before he learned how to operate a word processor, he had trouble with his typewritten assignments, but now he produces clean, attractive material.

Use punctuation consistent with that of the compound and complex sentences.

Other Methods of Combining Ideas

1. Simple sentences can often be combined by using a prepositional phrase.

> Dolly Parton wrote a song about a coat. The coat had many colors.
>
> Dolly Parton wrote a song about a coat *of many colors* (prepositional phrase).

2. To combine simple sentences, use an appositive, a noun phrase that immediately follows a noun or pronoun and renames it.

> Susan is the leading scorer on the team. Susan is a quick and strong player.
>
> Susan, *a quick and strong player*, is the leading scorer on the team.

3. Simple sentences can often be combined by dropping a repeated subject in the second sentence.

> Some items are too damaged for recycling. They must be disposed of.
>
> Some items are too damaged for recycling and must be disposed of.

4. Use a participial phrase, a group of words that include a participle which is a verbal that usually ends in *-ing* or *-ed.*

> John rowed smoothly. He reached the shore.
>
> *Rowing smoothly,* John reached the shore.

PARALLEL STRUCTURE

1. Parallelism means balancing one structure with another of the same kind—nouns with nouns, verbs with verbs, adjectives (words that can describe nouns) with adjectives, adverbs (words that can describe verbs) with adverbs, and so forth.

> *Men, women,* and *children* (nouns) *enjoy* the show and *return* (verbs) each year.
>
> She fell *in love* and *out of love* (phrases) in a few seconds.
>
> *She fell in love with him,* and *he fell in love with her* (clauses).

2. Faulty parallel structure is awkward and draws unfavorable attention to what is being said.

> *To talk* with his buddies and *eating* fast foods were his favorite pastimes (should be *Talking . . . and eating* or *To talk . . . and to eat*).

3. Some words signal parallel structure. All coordinating conjunctions (*for, and, nor, but, or, yet, so*) can give such signals.

> The weather is hot *and* humid.

> He purchased a Dodger Dog, *but* I chose Stadium Peanuts.

4. Combination words also signal the need for parallelism or balance. The most common ones are *either/or, neither/nor, not only/but also, both/and, whether/or.*

> We will *either* win this game *or* go out fighting (verb following each of the combination words).

Verbs

The twelve verb tenses are shown below. The irregular verb *drive* is used as the example. (See page 201 for irregular verbs.)

Simple Tenses

PRESENT I, we, you, they *drive.* He, she, it *drives.*	Present, may imply a continuation from past to future
PAST I, we, you, he, she, it, they *drove.*	Past
FUTURE I, we, you, he, she, it, they *will drive.*	Future

Perfect Tenses

PRESENT PERFECT I, we, you, they *have driven.* He, she, it *has driven.*	Completed recently in past, may continue to present
PAST PERFECT I, we, you, he, she, it, they *had driven.*	Prior to a specific time in the past
FUTURE PERFECT I, we, you, he, she, it, they *will have driven.*	At a time prior to a specific time in the future

Progressive Tenses

PRESENT PROGRESSIVE
I *am driving.*
He, she, it *is driving.*   In progress now
We, you, they *are driving.*

PAST PROGRESSIVE
I, he, she, it *was driving.*   In progress in the
We, you,they *were driving.*   past

FUTURE PROGRESSIVE
I, we, you, he, she, it, they *will be*   In progress in the
driving.   future

Perfect Progressive Tenses

PRESENT PERFECT PROGRESSIVE
I, we, you, they *have been*   In progress before
driving.   now or up to now
He, she, it *has been driving.*

PAST PERFECT PROGRESSIVE
I, we, you, he, she, it, they *had been*   In progress before
driving.   another event in the
                                             past

FUTURE PERFECT PROGRESSIVE
I, we, you, he, she, it, they *will*   In progress before
have been driving.   another event in the
                                             future

Past Participles

The past participle uses the helping verbs *has, have,* or *had* along with the past tense of the verb. For regular verbs, whose past tense ends in *-ed,* the past participle form of the verb is the same as the past tense.

Below is a list of some common regular verbs, showing the base form, the past tense, and the past participle. (The base form can also be used with such helping verbs as *can, could, do, does, did, may, might, must, shall, should, will,* and *would.*)

Regular Verbs

Base Form (Present)	Past	Past Participle
ask	asked	asked
answer	answered	answered
cry	cried	cried
decide	decided	decided
dive	dived (dove)	dived
finish	finished	finished
happen	happened	happened
learn	learned	learned
like	liked	liked
love	loved	loved
need	needed	needed
open	opened	opened
start	started	started
suppose	supposed	supposed
walk	walked	walked
want	wanted	wanted

Whereas **regular verbs** are predictable—having an *-ed* ending for past and past-participle forms—**irregular verbs,** as the term suggests, follow no definite pattern.

Below is a list of some common irregular verbs, showing the base form (present), the past tense, and the past participle.

Irregular Verbs

Base Form (Present)	Past	Past Participle
arise	arose	arisen
awake	awoke (awaked)	awaked
be	was, were	been
become	became	become
begin	began	begun
bend	bent	bent
blow	blew	blown
break	broke	broken
bring	brought	brought
buy	bought	bought

Base Form (Present)	Past	Past Participle
catch	caught	caught
choose	chose	chosen
cling	clung	clung
come	came	come
creep	crept	crept
deal	dealt	dealt
do	did	done
drink	drank	drunk
drive	drove	driven
eat	ate	eaten
feel	felt	felt
fight	fought	fought
fling	flung	flung
fly	flew	flown
forget	forgot	forgotten
freeze	froze	frozen
get	got	got (gotten)
go	went	gone
grow	grew	grown
have	had	had
know	knew	known
lead	led	led
leave	left	left
lose	lost	lost
mean	meant	meant
read	read	read
ride	rode	ridden
ring	rang	rung
shine	shone	shone
shoot	shot	shot
sing	sang	sung
sink	sank	sunk
sleep	slept	slept
slink	slunk	slunk
speak	spoke	spoken
spend	spent	spent
steal	stole	stolen
stink	stank (stunk)	stunk
sweep	swept	swept
swim	swam	swum
swing	swung	swung

Base Form (Present)	Past	Past Participle
take	took	taken
teach	taught	taught
tear	tore	torn
think	thought	thought
throw	threw	thrown
wake	woke (waked)	woken (waked)
weep	wept	wept
write	wrote	written

"Problem" Verbs

The following pairs of verbs are especially troublesome and confusing: *lie* and *lay*, *sit* and *set*, and *rise* and *raise*. One way to tell them apart is to remember which word in each pair takes a direct object. A direct object answers the question *whom* or *what* in connection with a verb. The words *lay*, *raise*, and *set* take a direct object.

> He *raised* the window. (He *raised* what?)

Lie, *rise*, and *sit*, however, cannot take a direct object. We cannot, for example, say "He rose the window." In the examples, the italicized words are objects.

Present Tense	Meaning	Past Tense	Past Participle	Example
lie	to rest	lay	lain	I lay down to rest.
lay	to place something	laid	laid	We laid the *books* on the table.
rise	to go up	rose	risen	The smoke rose quickly.
raise	to lift	raised	raised	She raised the *question*.
sit	to rest	sat	sat	He sat in the chair.
set	to place something	set	set	They set the *basket* on the floor.

Verb Tense

These rules about selecting a **tense** for certain kinds of writing are flexible, but you should be consistent, changing tense only for a good reason.

Usually you should select the present tense to write about literature.

> Moby Dick *is* a famous white whale.

Select the past tense to write about yourself (usually) or something historical (always).

> I *was* eighteen when I *decided* I *was* ready for independence.

Subject-Verb Agreement

The basic principle of **subject-verb agreement** of number is that if the subject is singular, the verb should be singular, and if the subject is plural, the verb should be plural.

> The *advantages* of that shoe *are* obvious.
> There *are* many *reasons* for his poor work.
> The *coach*, along with the players, *protests* the decision.
> The *price* of those shoes *is* too high.

Voice

The **active voice** (subject, active verb, and object) is usually preferred over the **passive voice** (subject as the receiver of action, with doer unstated or at the end of a prepositional phrase).

> She read the book. (active)
> The book was read by her. (passive)

PRONOUNS

A pronoun is a word that is used in place of a noun.

1. **Case** is the form a pronoun takes as it fills a position in a sentence.
2. **Subjective pronouns** are *I, he,* and *she* (singular), and *we* and *they* (plural). *Who* can be either singular or plural.
   Subject case pronouns can fill subject positions.

> *We* dance in the park.
> It was *she* who spoke. (referring back to and meaning the same as the subject)

3. **Objective case pronouns** are *me, him,* and *her* (singular); and *us* and *them* (plural). *Whom* can be either singular or plural.
   Objective case pronouns fill object positions.

   > We saw *her* in the library. (object of verb)
   >
   > They gave the results to *us*—Judy and *me.* (object of a preposition)

4. Three techniques are useful for deciding what pronoun case to use.
   a. If you have a compound element (such as a subject or object of a preposition), consider only the pronoun part.

   > They will visit Jim and (I, me). (Consider: They will visit me.)

   b. If the next important word after *who* or *whom* in a statement is a noun or pronoun, the word choice will be *whom;* otherwise, it will be *who.* Disregard qualifier clauses such as *It seems* and *I feel.*

   > The person *who* works hardest will win.
   >
   > The person *whom* judges like will win.
   >
   > The person *who,* we think, worked hardest won. (ignoring the qualifier clause)

   c. *Let's* is made up of the words *let* and *us* and means *"you let us";* therefore, when you select a pronoun to follow it, consider the two original words and select another object word—*me.*

   > Let's you and *me* go to town.

5. A **pronoun** agrees with its antecedent in person, number, and gender.
   a. Avoid needless shifting in **person,** which means shifting in point of view, such as from *I* to *you.*

   > *I* tried but *you* couldn't persuade her to return. (incorrect)
   >
   > *I* tried but *I* couldn't persuade her to return. (correct)

   b. Most problems with pronoun-antecedent agreement involve **number.** The principles are simple: If the antecedent (the word the pronoun refers back to) is singular, use a singular pronoun. If the antecedent is plural, use a plural pronoun.

   > Jim forgot *his* notebook.
   >
   > Many students cast *their* votes today.
   >
   > Someone lost *his* or *her* (not *their*) book.

c. The pronoun should agree with its antecedent in **gender,** if the gender of the antecedent is specific. Masculine and feminine pronouns are gender-specific: *he, him, she, her*. Others are neuter: *I, we, me, us, it, they, them, who, whom, that, which*. The words *who* and *whom* refer to people. *That* can refer to ideas, things, and people, but usually not to people. *Which* refers to ideas and things, but never to people. In order to avoid a perceived sex bias, most writers and speakers prefer to use *he or she* or *his or her* instead of just *he* or *his;* however many writers simply make antecedents plural.

> Everyone should work until *he* or *she* drops.

> People should work until *they* drop.

ADJECTIVES AND ADVERBS

1. **Adjectives** modify (describe) nouns and pronouns and answer the questions *Which one? What kind?* and *How many?*
2. **Adverbs** modify verbs, adjectives, or other adverbs and answer the questions *Where? When? Why?* and *How?* Most words ending in *-ly* are adverbs.
3. If you settle for a common word such as *good* or a slang word such as *neat* to characterize something you like, you will be limiting your communication. The more precise the word, the better the communication. Keep in mind, however, that anything can be overdone; therefore, use adjectives and adverbs wisely and economically.
4. For making comparisons, most adjectives and adverbs have three different forms: the positive (one), the comparative (two), and the superlative (three or more).
   a. Adjectives
      1. Add an *-er* to short adjectives (one or two syllables) to rank units of two.

         > Julian is *kinder* than Sam.

      2. Add an *-est* to short adjectives (one or two syllables) to rank units of more than two.

         > Of the fifty people I know, Julian is the *kindest*.

      3. Add the word *more* to long adjectives to rank units of two.

         > My hometown is *more beautiful* than yours.

4. Add the word *most* to long adjectives to rank units of three or more.

> My hometown is the *most beautiful* in all America.

5. Some adjectives are irregular in the way they change to show comparison.

> *good, better, best; bad, worse, worst*

b. Adverbs
For most adverbs, use the word *more* before the comparative form (two) and the word *most* before the superlative form (three or more).

> Jim performed *skillfully.* (modifier)
>
> Joan performed *more skillfully* (comparative modifier) than Joan.
>
> But Susan performed *most skillfully* (superlative modifier) of all.

5. **Avoid double negatives.** Words such as *no, not, none, nothing, never, hardly, barely,* and *scarcely* should not be combined.

> I *don't* have *no* time for recreation. (incorrect)
>
> I have no time for recreation. (correct)
>
> I don't have time for recreation. (correct)

6. Do not confuse adjectives (*bad*) with adverbs (*badly*).
7. A modifier that gives information but doesn't refer to a word already in the sentence is called a **dangling modifier.**

> *Walking down the street,* a snake startled me. (dangling)
>
> Walking down the street, I was startled by a snake. (correct)

8. A modifier that is placed so that it modifies the wrong word or words is called a **misplaced modifier.**

> The sick man went to a doctor *with a high fever.* (misplaced)
>
> The sick man with a high fever went to a doctor. (correct)

PUNCTUATION

1. The three marks of end punctuation are periods, question marks, and exclamation points.
   a. Periods
   Place a period after a statement.
   Place a period after common abbreviations.

b. Question Marks
Place a **question mark** at the end of a direct question.
Use a single question mark in sentence constructions that contain a double question—that is, a quoted question following a question.

> Mr. Martin said, "Did he say, 'Are we going?'"

Do *not* use a question mark after an indirect (reported) question.

> She asked me what caused the slide.

c. Exclamation Points
Place an **exclamation point** after a word or group of words that expresses strong feeling.
Do not overwork the exclamation point. Do not use double exclamation points.

2. The **comma** is used essentially to separate and to set off sentence elements.

a. Use a comma to separate main clauses joined by one of the coordinating conjunctions—*for, and, nor, but, or, yet, so.*

> We went to the game, *but* it was canceled.

b. Use a comma after introductory dependent clauses and long phrases (generally, four or more words is considered long).

> *Before she and I arrived,* the meeting was called to order.

c. Use a comma to separate words, phrases, and clauses in a series.

> He ran *down the street, across the park,* and into the arms of his father.

d. Use a comma to separate coordinate adjectives not joined by *and* that modify the same noun.

> I need a *sturdy, reliable* truck.

e. Use a comma to separate sentence elements that might be misread.

> Inside, the dog scratched his fleas.

f. Use commas to set off nonessential (unnecessary for meaning of the sentence) words, phrases, and clauses.

> Maria, who studied hard, will pass.

   g. Use commas to set off nouns used as direct address.

        Play it again, Sam.

   h. Use commas to separate the numbers in a date.

        June 4, 1965, is a day I will remember.

   i. Use commas to separate the city from the state. No comma is used between the state and the ZIP code.

        Walnut, CA 91789

   j. Use a comma following the salutation and the complementary closing in a letter (but in a business letter, use a colon after the salutation).

        Dear John,

        Sincerely,

   k. Use a comma in numbers to set off groups of three digits. However, omit the comma in dates and in long serial numbers, page numbers, and street numbers.

        The total assets were $2,000,000.

        I was born in 1980.

3. The semicolon indicates a stronger division than the comma. It is used principally to separate independent clauses within a sentence.

   a. Use a semicolon to separate independent clauses not joined by a coordinating conjunction.

        You must buy that car today; tomorrow will be too late.

   b. Use a semicolon between two independent clauses joined by a conjunctive adverb (such as *however, otherwise, therefore, similarly, hence, on the other hand, then, consequently, accordingly, thus*).

        It was very late; therefore, I remained at the hotel.

4. Quotation marks bring special attention to words.

   a. Quotation marks are used principally to set off direct quotations. A direct quotation consists of material taken from the written work or the direct speech of others; it is set off by double quotation marks. Single quotation marks are used to set off a quotation within a quotation.

        He said, "I don't remember if she said, 'Wait for me.'"

b. Use double quotation marks to set off titles of shorter pieces of writing such as magazine articles, essays, short stories, short poems, one-act plays, chapters in books, songs, and separate pieces of writing published as part of a larger work.

> The book *Literature: Structure, Sound, and Sense* contains a deeply moving poem entitled "On Wenlock Edge."
>
> Have you read "The Use of Force," a short story by William Carlos Williams?
>
> My favorite Elvis song is "Don't Be Cruel."

c. Punctuation with quotation marks follows definite rules.

1. A period or comma is always placed *inside* the quotation marks.

> Our assignment for Monday was to read Poe's "The Raven."
>
> "I will read you the story," he said. "It is a good one."

2. A semicolon or colon is always placed *outside* the quotation marks.

> He read Robert Frost's poem "Design"; then he gave the examination.

3. A question mark, exclamation point, or dash is placed *outside* the quotation marks when it applies to the entire sentence and *inside* the quotation marks when it applies to the material in quotation marks.

> He asked, "Am I responsible for everything?" (quoted question within a statement)
>
> Did you hear him say, "I have the answer"? (statement within a question)
>
> Did she say, "Are we ready?" (question within a question)
>
> She shouted, "Impossible!" (exclamation)
>
> "I hope—that is, I—" he began. (dash)

5. Italics (slanting type) is used to call special attention to certain words or groups of words. In handwriting or typing, such words are <u>underlined</u>.

a. Italicize (underline) foreign words and phrases that are still listed in the dictionary as foreign.

> *nouveau riche   Weltschmerz*

b. Italicize (underline) titles of books (except the Bible), long poems, plays, magazines, motion pictures, musical compositions, newspapers, works of art, names of aircraft, ships, and letters, figures, and words referred to by their own name.

War and Peace   *Apollo 12*   leaving *o* out of *sophomore*

6. The dash is used when a stronger break than the comma is needed. It can also be used to indicate a break in the flow of thought and to emphasize words (less formal than the colon in this situation).

Here is the true reason—but maybe you don't care.

English, French, history—these are the subjects I like.

7. The colon is a formal mark of punctuation used chiefly to introduce something that is to follow, such as a list, a quotation, or an explanation.

These cars are my favorites: Cadillac, Chevrolet, Buick, Oldsmobile, and Pontiac.

8. Parentheses are used to set off material that is of relatively little importance to the main thought of the sentence. Such material—numbers, parenthetical material, figures, supplementary material, and sometimes explanatory details—merely amplifies the main thought.

The years of the era (1961–1973) were full of action.

Her husband (she had been married only a year) died last week.

9. Brackets are used within a quotation to set off editorial additions or corrections made by the person who is quoting.

Churchill said: "It [the Yalta Agreement] contained many mistakes."

10. The apostrophe is used with nouns and indefinite pronouns to show possession, to show the omission of letters and figures in contractions, and to form the plurals of letters, figures, and words referred to as words.

man's coat, girls' clothes, *you're* (contraction of *you are*), five *and's*

11. The hyphen brings two or more words together into a single compound word. Correct hyphenation, therefore, is essentially a spelling problem rather than one of punctuation. Because the

hyphen is not used with any degree of consistency, consult your dictionary for current usage. Study the following as a beginning guide.

a. Use a hyphen to separate the parts of many compound words.

> about-face, go-between

b. Use a hyphen between prefixes and proper names.

> all-American, mid-November

c. Use a hyphen to join two or more words used as a single adjective modifier before a noun.

> first-class service, hard-fought game, sad-looking mother

d. Use a hyphen with spelled-out compound numbers up to ninety-nine and with fractions.

> twenty-six, two-thirds

Note: Dates, street addresses, numbers requiring more than two words, chapter and page numbers, time followed directly by *a.m.* or *p.m.*, and figures after a dollar sign or before measurement abbreviations are usually written as figures, not words.

CAPITALIZATION

In English, there are many conventions concerning the use of capital letters. Here are some of them.

1. Capitalize the first word of a sentence.
2. Capitalize proper nouns and adjectives derived from proper nouns.

Names of persons:
Edward Jones

Adjectives derived from proper nouns:
a Shakespearean sonnet, a Miltonic sonnet

Countries, nationalities, races, languages:
Germany, English, Spanish, Chinese

States, regions, localities, other geographical divisions:
California, the Far East, the South

Oceans, lakes, mountains, deserts, streets, parks:

Lake Superior, Fifth Avenue, Sahara Desert

Educational institutions, schools, courses:

Santa Ana College, Spanish 3, Joe Hill School, Rowland High School

Organizations and their members:

Boston Red Sox, Boy Scouts, Audubon Society

Corporations, governmental agencies or departments, trade names:

U.S. Steel Corporation, Treasury Department, White Memorial Library

Calendar references such as holidays, days of the week, months:

Easter, Tuesday, January

Historic eras, periods, documents, laws:

Declaration of Independence, Geneva Convention, First Crusade, Romantic Age

3. Capitalize words denoting family relationships when they are used before a name or substituted for a name.

> He walked with his nephew and Aunt Grace.
>
> but
>
> He walked with his nephew and his aunt.
>
> Grandmother and Mother are away on vacation.
>
> but
>
> My grandmother and my mother are away on vacation.

4. Capitalize abbreviations after names.

> Henry White, Jr.
>
> William Green, M.D.

5. Capitalize titles of themes, books, plays, movies, poems, magazines, newspapers, musical compositions, songs, and works of art. Do not capitalize short conjunctions and prepositions unless they come at the beginning or the end of the title.

> *Desire Under the Elms* *Terminator*
> *Last of the Mohicans* *Of Mice and Men*
> "Blueberry Hill"

6. Capitalize any title preceding a name or used as a substitute for a name. Do not capitalize a title following a name.

Judge Stone	Alfred Stone, a judge
General Clark	Raymond Clark, a general
Professor Fuentes	Harry Jones, the former president

Text Credits

Janet Castro, with Dan Cook and Cristina Garcia. "Spanglish Spoken Here." *Time,* July 11, 1988. Copyright © 1988 Time Inc. Reprinted by permission.

Carlos A. Chavez and Antonio H. Rodriguez, "*La Vida Loca:* Crazy Life, Crazy Death." *Los Angeles Times,* August 17, 1995. Reprinted by permission of the authors.

Seymour Feshback and Bernard Weiner, "Total Institutions" from *Personality.* © 1991 D. C. Heath and Co. Reprinted by permission.

Fourteen Numbered Points from the MLA web site, "Citing Sources from the World Wide Web." Reprinted by permission of the Modern Language Association of America.

Martin Gotfried, "Rambos of the Road." *Newsweek,* September 8, 1986. Reprinted by permission of the author.

Mary Ann Hogan, "Why We Carp and Harp." Copyright © 1992 by *Los Angeles Times.* Reprinted by permission.

Vance Horn, "Japanese Tea Ceremony." Reprinted with permission of *The Olympian,* Olympia, Washington, April 4, 1987.

Marcus Mabry, "Living in Two Worlds," from *Newsweek on Campus* (Supplement), April 1998. Author of *White Bucks and Black-Eyed Peas: Coming of Age Black in White America* (Scribners, 1995). Reprinted by permission of the author.

Louis Nizer, "How About Low-Cost Drugs for Addicts?" *New York Times,* June 8, 1986. Copyright © 1986 by The New York Times Company. Reprinted by permission.

Gary Soto, "The Pie," from *A Summer Life.* © 1990 by University Press of New England. Reprinted by permission.

INDEX